quadrille

50 Recipes that Bring all the Flavour and Fun

TACOS

Nud Dudhia + Chris Whitney

Photography by Kris Kirkham

TACOS ARE LIFE

Our love affair with tacos has not wavered since we wrote our first book in 2016. In fact, it has intensified and bordered on obsessive. We have travelled to Mexico 15 times in the last seven years, visiting as many regions, cities and taco vendors as physically possible to further our understanding of the deliciously complex and varied world of tacos. Our journeys have taken us through back streets, jungles, mountains, rivers, coastlines and border towns, and at each stop and with each taco eaten, we have learnt something new – from preparations of salsas, to techniques of cooking meat and entirely new dishes (beef eye taco, anyone?), our taco odyssey has continued to reaffirm our love of the incredible food and culture of Mexico. Over the last seven years we've shared our love of tacos with thousands of people across the world via pop ups and events and opened taquerías in Manchester, Liverpool and even Oslo, Norway. It's almost impossible to estimate how many tacos we've actually sold, but we're definitely in the millions by now...

BUT, WHAT EXACTLY *IS* A TACO?

In Spanish, a taco means plug... A taco fills that hole in your stomach when you're hungry, whether at work, grabbing a bite on the go, shopping or any other time of the day.

Tacos are a pre-Hispanic food consisting of a circular tortilla (corn or flour) folded and filled with vegetables, meat, fish and seafood, insects or beans. The fillings are cooked using a variety of methods, such as confit (cooked in its own fat), guisado (stewed), milanese (fried), al carbón (grilled over coal), crudo (raw), al vapor (steamed), al pastor (spit roasted) and a la plancha (on the flat top). Throughout Mexico these techniques are used by taqueros (taco chefs) uniquely and deftly to create mouth-wateringly delicious little bites of food that are served at high speed and low cost.

The taco genre is ever evolving in its vocabulary and a new style is unveiled almost every day. The natural movement of people to, from and throughout Mexico ensures influences from global cuisine are infused with time-honoured traditions and techniques to constantly reimagine what tacos are and can be.

The life of a taquero is tough, and competition to be the best is fuelled by machismo, inventiveness and virility. Stop by most taco stands anywhere in Mexico and you'll see a brave display of showmanship to attract customers and display skill, from carving meat from a fire-throwing spit to deft skills of chopping and delivering meats. These streets are lined with a myriad of craftsmen who have spent their entire lives perfecting their particular style of taco, from al pastor to birria, barbacoa to suadero, canasta to carnitas. The vocabulary of the taco genre is so vast and varied, a lifetime would not be long enough to take in every local, regional or national subtlety!

One thing you realize in Mexico is that tacos are culture and tacos are life. People don't eat to live there; they have a passion for food that is so deeply ingrained into society, almost everybody talks, thinks and procrastinates about it all of the time. As you ramble the streets of any city or town, the smell of pork fat, corn and stewing meats permeate your skin, clothes and tastebuds. Even when you think you are full, there's always room for uno más (one more).

HOW TO TACO?

There aren't very many rules when it comes to eating tacos, apart from no fork and no knives, please... The standard formula, however, starts with the tortilla followed by meat, vegetables or beans, then some kind of salsa, coriander, onions and lime. This is the structure that most taqueros follow, and in Mexico you'll almost always be asked the question, 'con todo?' (served complete, or as the chef designs, with coriander, onion and salsa), and your answer should always be, of course, yes!

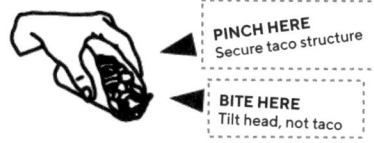

PINCH HERE
Secure taco structure

BITE HERE
Tilt head, not taco

This is the style that breddos has tried to embody on our journey – the taco as a complete dish with layered balance. From the umami-rich proteins topped with the sharp and fiery salsas, to the freshness of raw onion, coriander and, of course, lime, the taco becomes something more than a sum of it parts when assembled in this tried and tested manner.

This is by no means a rigid philosophy, merely our interpretation, where the tortilla is viewed as a tiny, 12cm, edible plate, able to provide the basis for combinations and concoctions that transport you to Mexico, via south east Asia and beyond, and this is something that is reflected in the recipes you find in this book.

Hopefully these recipes will provide a delicious starting point from which you can embark upon, or continue on your own taco odyssey, adding your own personal take to the vast, ever changing pantheon of Mexican food.

TACO

TRAIL

THE FIRST TRIP
NYC, LA, DF

We decided that our first trip would consist of spending four or five days in three cities that were creating the greatest things in the name of the taco. We embarked on an impressive amount of research and came up with a terrifyingly long list of where we had to eat over the course of the trip. To get through our list, we worked out that we were going to be averaging 10 spots a day. Still we soldiered on, risking our own health, souls, relationships and potentially a nasty case of gout, all for the greater good.

FIRST STOP, NYC

A very good friend of ours picked us up from the airport for a catch-up lunch at her house in New Jersey before we travelled into Manhattan. Although we had mentioned our insane eating schedule to our hosts, after half an hour Nat's husband James shouted that lunch was served and out came a 10oz porterhouse steak with the full works. This pretty much set the tone for the rest of the trip.

Feeling enormously full and not a little bit tipsy, we jumped (or rather lugged ourselves) on the train to Manhattan. The hotel we were staying at was The Jane, located on the edge of the Meatpacking District. Our room was so small that we had to take it in turns to get ready, with one person standing in the hotel corridor outside. From this point onwards, we decided not to spend much time in the room, for both of our sanities.

To kick off, our first dinner was at The Black Ant on the Lower East Side. We had been keen to try this place for ages, as they were known for having developed an entirely modern take on Mexican food. We then went on to having a couple more suppers before calling it a night.

The next few days passed by in a bit of a gluttonous blur. By day we would hit up all the taco joints, like Choza in Gotham West, Tacos No. 1 in West Chelsea, and markets such as the newly opened Gansevoort Market in the Meatpacking District. At each place we visited we would order the majority of the menu; this involved a hell of a LOT of braised meat. By night we would hit up the restaurants and the bars: Danny Bowien's Mission Cantina, Alex Stupak's Empellón and Empellón Cocina. In terms of bars, Attaboy on the Lower East Side, formerly Milk and Honey, was a knockout. It was at this point that our time in New York started to get a little hazy in the way that only New York can. The whole city is so compact and incredibly intense, and our hotel room only compounded both of these senses.

CALIFORNIA, CALIFORNIA

It was time to get on a plane and head west to California. Neither of us had been there, but we were armed with the next cracking list of where to eat thanks to a local guy. We landed at LAX and hired a car, a convertible Mustang, obviously (and not, as some would have it, a hairdresser's car). The first thing that struck us about LA was its sheer size. It was absolutely massive. Not just in geographical terms – even its roads were vast and everything was low rise and sprawling. It was the antithesis of New York.

The next day we woke up early. There were some serious tacos to discover, after all. We jumped into the car, put the roof down and headed out to pursue tacos anew, and felt the first licks of the Californian sun tickle our skin. First stop was Guisados in east LA. N.B. At this point we should mention that after four days of eating non-stop tacos, something happens to a man. Your physiology starts to change. It's as if your body starts to sense the potential fat content in the air, and if you walk past braising meat, you have a physical reaction. Which is pretty much your body rejecting what's about to be put in it. We arrived at Guisados and as soon as we opened the door we were hit with that smell. Braised meat. It was at this point that our knees started to knock and we both wanted to cry. Against our instincts and our bodies' wishes, we entered.

We got chatting to the owner. We explained what we were doing in the US and he insisted we try... everything. It was just 10a.m. After eating all his fantastic tacos, we went next door to his brother's shop where they nixtamalized all of the corn for the tortillas in-house. He explained that 'guisado' meant 'braised'. Duh! This became one of the more useful bits of knowledge that we learnt on the whole trip...

The level of eating continued apace. We would drive for 20 minutes then stop for some tacos, drive, tacos, drive, tacos... The evening of the second day arrived, and the main event, dinner at Animal. This was one of the restaurants we were most looking forward to and it did not disappoint; once we had found it, that is. There's no name on the door. The menu was vast and it's one of those rare places where you could eat every single thing on it. Dish after dish of amazing-ness arrived and was duly demolished. While we were eating we noticed a bar across the road that also had no name on the door; it just had a couple of burly looking chaps outside. We asked a newly acquired friend what the deal was and he explained that it was called 'No name' and was, at that moment, LA's hottest bar. We queried as to our chances of getting in. 'You can try' was the response. So, of course, we walked across the road, where Nud put on his poshest accent and explained we were from out of town. The guy disappeared inside, a few minutes later he came out and ushered us in. From here on in things got a bit blurry. We vaguely remember being stood next to Justin Timberlake, boring one of the guys from Tame Impala to death and having an in-depth chat on feminism with his friend, a very pretty lead singer from a band whose name escaped us. Apparently we went to Soho House at some point that night. We definitely went to one club where the girls were so pretty we had to leave. At some point we had an almighty argument somewhere on Sunset Strip and went our separate ways.

We both woke up in the morning feeling more than a little sheepish. Still, we had a mission to complete. So we loaded ourselves back into the car and headed to find a place simply called 'the best fish tacos in Ensenada'. The last thing either of us wanted to do was to go and eat tacos, but this was our MO, our raison d'être; the entire reason why we were here, so we proceeded to order two of everything on offer. Taking the first bite with trepidation, what occurred was entirely unexpected. They were a revelation! So simple, just fish battered and fried in a massive wok right in front of you, seasoned to perfection with a choice of salsas. It was so good we ordered more.

We jumped back into the car and drove back down the hill, and about 200 yards down the road we saw a truck, Ricky's Tacos, parked on the side of the road. This was also on our hit list so we stopped and ordered more fish tacos. Fantastic again. We were getting into our stride now. Next stop was downtown to the arts district. We arrived at Grand Central Market, filled with authentic Mexican stands selling both produce and the finished articles: tacos, quesadillas, enchiladas. There were stands selling moles, all manner of chillies, fresh and dried tortillas. This place brought home how seriously California, and indeed the US in general, takes its Mexican food.

We then decided to check out Guerrilla Tacos, a truck doing really interesting things with their food, exactly what we had come here to eat. It was brilliant, and chef Wes Avila's twist on classic Mexican fare was really inspiring. However, at this point, we had started hallucinating from too many calories and urgently needed a respite from our eating agenda. Nothing fancy, stay in, pizza, movie, refreshed and ready to go the next day. At about 11.30p.m. Nud burst into action.

"Right, c'mon, we've got to go."

"What?!" I replied.

"Kogi, they're gonna be at such and such place in 30 minutes. C'mon, sort yourself out."

However much we didn't want to go, and we really didn't, these were the guys that started everything. The original food truck that kicked everything off. Roy Choi is a demi-god in the LA and global food scene and has a fleet of trucks that tweet where they are going. To go to LA and not seek them out, given what we do, would have been crazy. We fired the street name into the sat nav and sped off. We arrived at a nondescript corner and parked up. No sign of the truck. Moments later, the famous truck rolled into view, instantly recognizable. What seemed like five seconds later an enormous queue appeared snaking off into the distance. Where the hell had everyone come from? Thankfully, we were at the front of the queue. The famous Korean short-rib tacos, black jack quesadillas... the works. The guy at the front was the man himself, Roy bloody Choi! We were so full that we could only manage a few bites of each taco but it was enough to confirm that the hype was totally justified.

Strangely, when we woke up, breakfast wasn't the first thing on our minds. Besides, we had a brunch date with Chris, the illusive dude who had supplied tips for our hit list, at a restaurant that we'd never heard of, but had insisted was unmissable. So, we headed south east towards Corazón y Miel, which turned out to be in a Latino neighbourhood that had a massive Mexican hypermarket that sold absolutely everything in the world. We wandered round agog at its size before Nud got us booted out for filming a shelf full of tortillas. We headed over the road and in through another unnamed door into a restaurant that was buzzing. We'd never met Chris before, as we had communicated solely through email, so it was a real pleasure to meet the guy who'd helped us out with so many recommendations for the trip. It turned out that Chris worked in the movie business and that he was currently working on a project that was particularly close to his heart. The premise of the show was to follow individual chefs who were doing particularly brilliant things and to showcase their journey.

We woke up on our final morning to yet another perfect, sunshine-filled LA day. We had a few hours to kill before we jumped on another plane that would take us to Mexico City, so we drove up to the Griffith Observatory to have a look at the spectacular views.

What. A. City.

NEXT STOP, DF MEXICO

As we flew over Mexico City, we couldn't get over the sheer scale of the place. This was in a completely different league, even to LA. We flew over the city for half an hour before we landed.

Upon arrival, we hopped in a cab and headed over to the apartment we had rented, situated in La Condesa, one of the cooler neighbourhoods and the home to many of the restaurants we had on our list. We had done a ton of research and curated a formidable list of restaurants, stalls and markets that we needed to visit. Due to our relatively relaxed last few days in LA, a kind of complacency had set in. This was about to be shattered into a million tiny pieces over the next few days...

The first morning was spent navigating the maze that is La Condesa, stopping at every taquería we could find and ordering the whole menu. This really was a beautiful neighbourhood, with tree-lined streets, small parks in the middle of islands, and squares boasting amazing architecture. The vast majority of the tacos in DF are very traditional; guisado or chorizo garnished with onions and a touch of coriander (cilantro) with a choice of salsas (normally three). DF is also the home of tacos al pastor. If you've not come across these, they're tacos that are cut from a large mass of marinated pork shoulder cutlets piled on top of one another on a revolving trompo (picture a chicken doner). On the top of the spit is a whole pineapple and when all the meat is shaved into your taco, the taquero cuts and flicks a chunk of pineapple on top. Their dexterity is utterly impressive; they could probably flick a piece into a beer bottle on a table 10 feet away. Its origins come from Lebanese settlers who combined their native techniques with the established way of doing things in Mexico.

We then decided to head out to the bars that lined the streets of La Roma. We turned into a massive road and lo and behold there were bars and restaurants everywhere, some of which looked much more salubrious than others. We spent an evening getting to know the bars and taquerías of La Roma. There were fantastic drinks, including the best margarita either of us had ever had, in a lovely bar that we completely forgot to get the name of (handy eh?). We decided to call it a night. On our way back (slightly worse for wear), we walked past a doorway with lots of people standing outside, alongside a couple of intimidating bouncers. The doorway was nothing special, a simple light leading to an old wooden staircase.

Given the clientele, this place warranted further inspection. After confirming that it was indeed a bar (always a good idea), we climbed up the winding staircase and what greeted us at the top was staggering. Between two higher buildings they'd built a conservatory that was about 40 feet high, with sliding glass panels that opened the place up to the heavens. There were massive palm trees around the dimly lit room where all of DF's bright young things sat. It was a thing to behold. You couldn't help but be seduced by everything about it. It turned out that this place was called Romita Comedor. We managed to work this out after about an hour of staring at a 20-foot neon sign only 6 feet from where we were sitting with the bar's name emblazoned on it. It was time to go.

The next day we decided to hit the markets. We headed towards the biggest of them all, La Merced. The size of the markets was absolutely staggering. You could wander around for half an hour and you wouldn't even have got through the crisp section. Piles and piles of cleanly prepped vegetables sat stacked up in perfect symmetry and order. We could easily have lost a day in the place. One of the other benefits is that the market is also rammed full of mini-food courts, so you're never more than a hundred yards from a taco. By the time it came to lunch, there was a place that Nud wanted to check out

called Contramar, located in La Condesa. The place was humming with people and waiters alike. As luck would have it, one of the highly coveted outside tables became available just as we were at the front of the queue, a perfect place to watch the great and good flow in and out of the restaurant. Despite initially having to force ourselves to open our mouths, we managed to demolish a fair few of their star turns.

That night we had the main event: Pujol, which was regarded as the most forward-thinking Mexican restaurant in the world. We were quite literally champing at the bit to see what the chef, Enrique Olvera, had got. Upon sitting down, we were whisked through course after course of food that pushed boundary after boundary. The smoked ant was superb, as were the signature new and old moles. One mole was freshly made, the other was just over a year old and was fed every day so it continually gained richness and intensity.

The next day we had the pleasure of being shown around the city by Maurizio and his girlfriend Franci, who were both locals. Maurizio, an artist, had grown up in DF and had returned after living all over the world. The first place they took us to was an old cantina next to a massive park, a true vision of old-school Mexico. We had to sit in the lounge area, as women were not allowed in the main restaurant. (Like we said, old school.)

We then continued bopping round from place to place, enjoying the lack of responsibility that comes with being shown around. Cafés, bars, taquerías; all were taken in on this whistle-stop tour. As late afternoon turned into an early dusk-filled hazy evening, Maurizio decided to take us for the perfect margarita.

It was a trek, he explained, but well worth it and something he used to do with his family. Perfect margarita? He didn't get any complaints from us. After an hour in the cab we started to notice the houses around us getting bigger and bigger and disappearing behind more and more giant gates with bodyguards outside.

Upon arrival, we piled out of our battered little cab and walked through the entrance into a garden that would make the Beverly Hills Country Club look cheap. This was without a doubt the smartest place we had ever been to. We went to sit in a garden filled with candles and lanterns and Maurizio ordered four margaritas. They brought out frozen glasses with limes, along with miniature silver wine buckets, full of ice, on top of which sat a silver flask containing the hallowed margarita. All of this pomp and splendour certainly added to the experience.

When it reached dinnertime we headed back to La Roma, and Maurizio's favourite restaurant, run by a friend of his who incidentally used to work at Pujol. We entered Máximo Bistrot and were greeted like old friends. It was a cute little place, with a very low-key and buzzy vibe.

This turned out to be one of the best meals of the trip, sensational food and atmosphere and a brilliant way to round off our epic trip.

———————

During the summer of 2015, we were approached by the folks at Quadrille, who asked if we'd like to write our first book.

"Us? What? Really?" was what initially sprung to mind.

We had a lot on at that point, planning the route we wanted breddos Tacos to take, and the thought of writing a book was daunting to say the least. How do we even start? How do we fill it?

"If we're doing a book, mate, we need to go on another trip," said Nud.

"Well then, let's do the book," I said.

TRIP NO.2 THE SECOND TACO COMING

This time around we wanted to check out the places that were doing the most inventive things with, yes you guessed it, tacos. Top of the list was Baja California and in particular Ensenada and the Valle de Guadalupe, the Mexican wine country. Next on the list was San Francisco. A place that had been seared into our memories by virtue of Hollywood and somewhere neither of us had been to before but were both itching to go to, however contentious that would be with our girlfriends... Finally, and fortuitously, we were going to go back to LA. Too great a city, too good an opportunity to miss...

SAN FRAN

We arrived in downtown San Francisco, all hustle and bustle and a hell of a lot warmer than we had expected. First place on this trip list was State Bird Provisions. Everyone that we knew or had ever met raved about this place, so we had to go and chance the massive queue that was apparently a permanent fixture. We turned up expecting to see the infamous line snaking down the road. Nothing. By sheer fluke we'd managed to time it perfectly and we just strolled on in. The method of serving was unlike anywhere else we had experienced. You got your menu, ordered the dishes you wanted, and trolleys would come round with small plates that you could add to your meal.

Being completely unaccustomed to this style of dining, we went in hard, taking a small plate from the trolley nearly every time one was offered to us. By the time the food we ordered arrived, we were absolutely stuffed. Everything we ate was delicious, not a dud note to be found, from the Kung Pao beef tongue to the deep fried garlic bread filled with burrata. Full to the brim, the only thing for it was to go and find some bars and see what the nightlife of this famous city had to offer. Being the first night we got a little bit too excited and what ensued was another one of those lost evenings.

Suffice to say we managed to try the entire list at a bar whose name still escapes us, and we both recall spending some time in a bar that resembled a pirate ship.

The next few days were spent wandering around the Mission District, trying all of the taco joints that were recommended to us. If we're completely honest, nothing really stood out and captured our imagination – in terms of authenticity, the tacos were great, but we were hungry for more. We were looking for food that was changing the game.

Our best evening in San Fran started at Al's Place, voted the USA's best restaurant by *Bon Appetit* in 2015. The flavours that chef Aaron London created, coupled with the presentation and stark white dining room, created a truly unforgettable meal.

That was it for San Francisco. Maybe we did it wrong, maybe there were other spots that we missed that would have blown us away. One thing's for sure, San Francisco, great city that it was, really didn't suck us in and beguile us like LA had done the year before. Speaking of which, it was time to head back to the city of angels...

LA TAKE II

We picked up a car (another convertible Mustang, naturally) and headed to our usual hotel in West Hollywood. On this trip we were actually going to be in LA twice, three days on this stint and then back again for a couple of nights after Baja and before our return to London. This afforded us the luxury of not having to go too bonkers. We could revisit some of our favourite haunts from the last trip and check out any newcomers that fell into our new remit. Bliss.

Over the course of the next few days we went back to Animal (just as brilliant), best fish tacos in Ensenada (good but not as good as we had remembered) and Guerrilla Tacos (awesome as always). There were new places that we tried like Jon & Vinny's, a pizza place from the guys that own Animal and Son of a Gun, and Night Market Song out in Silverlake, LA's hipster neighbourhood. There were a few places that we had meant to go to last time but couldn't make it to. One of those places was Petty Cash Taquería on Melrose. This time we had a specific reason to go, as we had made contact with a guy called Bill Esparza. Bill is THE authority on all things Mexican, particularly tacos and mezcal, and his blog has a huge following. It turned out he was doing a mezcal tasting class at Petty Cash and we said we'd come down and join in, kill two birds with one stone.

We arrived and sat down, ordering a few bits and pieces: fish tacos, chips and guac with uni, or sea urchin. Bill then arrived with his cohort of mezcal heads ready for what was to be an important date in mezcal's history. We said our hellos and got stuck into the tasting session[1]. They'd managed to get hold of what's regarded in these circles as the best mezcal in the world, and something that had never been allowed into the States before, and they had got hold of all six variants, representing the different agave plants. Over the course of the next hour or so we tasted 10 or more mezcals, and unlike any other tasting we've been to, there wasn't much spitting out going on. Once the tasting had finished Bill stayed around for a chat and it turned out that he was going to be in Tijuana for the Baja food festival, a celebration of the culinary prowess of the area. He'd be there with a load of the chefs whose restaurants and trucks we'd been visiting on our trips. We hadn't planned on going to Tijuana but this was worth changing our plans for. We said our goodbyes, exchanged details and made arrangements to meet that Friday.

1 Mezcal is still a bit under appreciated in London, but it was fascinating to learn about the techniques used to make it. Tequila, for instance, is made from one particular type of agave plant and in one region within Mexico. Mezcal, on the other hand, is made from many varieties and all over Mexico, though predominantly in Oaxaca and Chihuahua; this gives rise to a diversity and complexity that belies its popularity and really can be compared to whisky in its complexity.

The final day of this first stint in LA came. We'd arranged to meet an old-school breddo of ours, Al, who happened to be in town, so this had the potential to get messy. The breddos reunited; we headed to Melrose Avenue, where lots of new cocktail joints had popped up, and we embarked on something approaching a bar crawl. While this was fun, it was not entirely sensible, as we had a long drive down to Mexico the following day.

I woke up to my alarm screaming and a hotel room littered with bottles and cans. Clearly the party had come back to the hotel. The combination of a thumping head, having to get our shit together and now the added pain of having to clean the bomb site that was our hotel room, was not ideal. It transpired I'd passed out while Nud and Al carried on getting stuck in at the hotel (most out of character and a bit of a role reversal). While I'd felt better, it was nothing a coffee and a bottle of water wouldn't sort out. Nud, on the other hand, was in all sorts of trouble. In the 15 years we'd known one another, I had never seen him so bad.

The sole reason for us having to get out of bed early was that we had a dinner reservation at a restaurant called Corazón de Tierra at 6.30p.m. that evening. The issue was that it was a four-hour drive to the border, another hour to cross, God knows how long to rent another car, a further two hours' drive to Ensenada, check in, sort ourselves out and then drive the 45km (28 miles) into the Valle de Guadalupe where Corazón de Tierra was situated. There wasn't a lot of margin for error, so this was not the most auspicious start...

We lugged our stuff into the car, dropped the roof down and headed out in the direction of Mexico via Highway 101. Immediately, Nud curled up in the fetal position in the passenger seat. I thought I would leave him be, but once he regained consciousness, I'd give him hell. (That's what friends are for, of course.)

The drive down to San Diego went almost without a hitch (only a couple of stops for Nud to throw up). We got to the border and parked up. Nud assured me that while he still felt terrible, he was through the worst of it. I was feeling very little sympathy at this point, as I knew that I would now have to drive the whole way – driving in the States was one thing, but driving in Mexico was going to be a different kettle of fish altogether. It turned out to be a very smooth process; we passed immigration and were weaving our way through the barriers, staring directly at the final bag check security and the guards' gleaming AK47s, when Nud suddenly started looking panicked and walking around in circles. Oh Christ, not now I thought. I could see his eyes moistening. He covered his mouth and started convulsing. He then projectile vomited in the middle of the hall, which was completely empty barring the guards with the aforementioned big shiny guns... and me. Thinking on my feet, I started shouting sorry to anyone who'd listen while trying to hastily wipe up the contents of Nud's stomach with a t-shirt I had pulled out from my bag. The guards quickly ushered us out of the hall, where we were greeted by sunlight pouring through an open door, above which read a sign: 'Welcome to Mexico'.

What an entrance...

HELLO MEXICO! WE'RE BACK...

The road that took us down through Baja was absolutely staggering. We drove along the cliff, staring out across the Pacific. It was stupendously beautiful. (Unfortunately, Nud missed it all – as he had resumed the recovery position.)

Finally, after a very long day of driving, we got to Ensenada and found the hotel. 'Interesting' would have been one word for it, though there are others far more appropriate. Our room, while clean, looked and felt like terrible things had happened in it and, given the proliferation of 'mujeres de la noche' touting their 'wares' outside our window, we didn't doubt this was the case. Amazingly, we had made the journey in great time and had an hour to sort ourselves out. Nud jumped into bed and pulled the covers over his head. I had started to feel something approaching sympathy by this point. Torturing him would be no fun at all in this state, he was a sitting duck.

When the time came to leave, we headed back up the road, the way we had come, and turned into the Valle de Guadalupe. This is the major wine area in Mexico and it had started to build quite a good reputation for itself; the terroir mirrored that of southern California. Vineyards stretched as far as the eye could see, in every direction. As magical as this vista was, there was a slight issue – all of the restaurants were located on vineyards which had no real addresses. If you didn't know where you were going, you were screwed. We found that the best way to locate anything was to find the town that it was near, El Porvenir in this case, and hope to drive around and find a sign. After a lot of driving down twisty vineyard lanes, we arrived with a minute to spare. The restaurant, Corazón de Tierra ('Heart of the Land'), was located at a vineyard called Vena Cava. We entered by a ramp through some nondescript buildings that had big oil lanterns guiding our way.

It was then that we entered one of the most beautiful restaurants we had ever seen. Huge timbers jutted out of the ground, about 25 feet (7.6 metres) high, and in between them sat enormous panes of glass. The end of the building was completely open and looked out over the gardens which grew all of the restaurant's produce, and the view extended down to the valley, where the sun was setting over the Pacific. The kitchen at the other end was built out of rocks, with a huge fire pit at its centre. It was breathtaking. We don't know if it was the after-effects of the previous night or the fact that we were knackered but it made us both really emotional.

The first thing we were offered was a glass of wine, all produced in-house, of course. Given his fragile state, Nud opted out of this and asked the bamboozled sommelier for a large glass of milk. Still, that meant that I could drink all the wine and Nud could drive home. Every cloud...

The meal was faultless. Incredible produce and cleverly put together by a brilliant team of chefs. This was what we'd travelled all this way for: modern interpretations of classic Mexican food, with exceptional local produce. A true highlight of the whole trip. A stunning experience all round and if you can go, you should.

Before we left Ensenada, we had a full day of eating planned. Ensenada is one of the most incredible places for seafood on earth. In fact, eight out of 10 of the world's most expensive seafood come from here – abalone, urchin and tuna. Until a couple of decades ago, these seafood were all exported to Japan, but then Mexican chefs, such as Benito Molina (Manzanilla), opened restaurants that celebrated the diversity of the local catch. In Ensenada, we were in the eye of the hurricane of our research trip.

First stop was Mariscos La Guerrerense, from Ms. Sabina Bandera, a world famous street stall. She was celebrated for her seafood tostadas and rightly so. Her guys turned up with bags of urchins, clams, oysters and sea snails, all pulled straight out of the sea and prepped ceviche-style before our eyes, along with 30 of her salsas to choose from. It was utterly sensational, and neither of us had tasted flavours like it before. Sea urchins with pismo clams and chilli peanut oil, fresh and creamy oysters – it was a total revelation. The next stop was Tacos El Fenix. These guys were famous for their Baja fish tacos; freshly fried fish, shredded cabbage, pico and salsa. It's often said that it's the simplest things that bring you the most pleasure, and this was a classic example.

The final stop before lunch was to El Pizón to visit Alan Pasiano, who sells uni tostadas at the far end of the town. What's more remarkable, however, was this guy's story. Until a few years ago, the majority of the food caught and landed in Ensenada would be transported to Japan. It was seen as the epicentre of the sea urchin universe and this guy was the uni (as it's called in Japan) king. He travelled to Japan and became the uni king there too. This guy was a rock star but he became addicted to drugs and disappeared for 20 years. He then came out of this torpor, moved back to Ensenada and restarted his original plan all over again. Unbelievable.

It was now just about time for lunch and we had a booking at Manzanilla, one of the most celebrated restaurants in the area. We opted for the 10-course tasting menu that included Smoked abalon and Bluefin tuna. We then managed to squeeze one

more lunch in at Deckman's, an impossibly romantic open-air restaurant under a tree in a vineyard that was wasted on us, before heading back up towards Tijuana.

We had arranged to meet Bill in the lobby of the Grand Hotel Tijuana where the conference was taking place. All the chefs were in town to do demos and cook a big banquet on Saturday to showcase the produce and culinary philosophy of this region. It was a who's who of chefs at the forefront of the cutting edge of Mexican food in California. There was Wes Avila from Guerrilla Tacos, Carlos Salgado from Taco María in Orange County, Ray Garcia from Broken Spanish and B.S. Taquería, Eddy Ruiz, co-owner of Corazón y Miel, oh, and us. The plan was that Bill would take all of us to some spots he knew exemplified particular styles of tacos, which we would never have found ourselves in a million years.

The first place we went to served the best tacos al pastor that the city had to offer. The place was buzzing with locals, people coming and going the whole time. The second joint was a tiny little place with a simple wood grill and a tiny ramshackle extraction unit. There were about 15 of us and we joked that these guys would be completely in the weeds with the amount of orders they were about to receive. Not a bit of it. They went from doing nothing to slinging out tacos at a rate that was scarcely believable. These were some of the best carne asada tacos we had ever tasted. At this point the group decided that we all needed beer, so we headed to a night-time container yard. There was an incredible selection of craft beers, much of it brewed in situ. We sampled more than a few before the party started to break up. One of the plans was to stay up until 3a.m. as there was a stall that had its opening hours from 3 to 4.30a.m. on a Friday and Saturday. Unfortunately, we didn't manage to stay up that late, so we're unable to report on what kind of alchemy this guy was up to, to enable this fantasy lifestyle.

The next morning, we headed back up the coast to LA, completely inspired by our trip. We had seen what we needed to see and were bursting with ideas, not just for food but for everything we wanted to achieve. This had been a classic trip. Baja was majestic and California was as great as ever. Now it was time to do some real work and try to do justice to all we'd seen[2].

---

2 (We still get this nagging feeling that one day we will get found out. Surely, we can't enjoy what we do for a living this much. If it does all go to pot and breddos Tacos is no more, then at least this book will stand as some sort of testament to us that this did all actually happen.)

OUR
RELATIONSHIP

NUD ON CHRIS

Chris and I met at university through our wider friendship group. Back then we had other things on our mind and, to be honest, food was not one of them. We both moved to London from Manchester around the same time and shared a flat in Dalston. It was to be at least eight years until the idea of opening a food business dawned upon us.

Chris and I are very different beasts, with very different skill sets. While I manage the culinary and 'brand' related jobs, Chris looks after the finances and, more importantly, the building of our sites. The latter is where Chris really excels – he has a very logical mind and craft skills to build our transient sites over a very short period of time. He also has the best handwriting in street food, although I still can't read most of it. Ultimately, as business partners, our skills complement each other rather than oppose or conflict and that is the key to our creative and operational output. I think we both agree that we're very lucky to have each other as partners and friends.

CHRIS ON NUD

The first thing that needs to be said and appreciated is that all of the recipes, and everything that we've ever done in terms of food, has come from Nud's head. I have never met anyone who thinks about food as much as he does!

We couldn't be any more different if we tried, but the fact that we both approach everything from different angles is one of the biggest strengths we have and I don't think either of us would change it. Although, sometimes we could kill each other. Most of the time, we're laughing and joking, but we're always trying to push things forward. It's a privilege working with such a talented guy, my best mate, my breddo.

THE LARDER

In this section you'll find most of the ingredients you'll need to make the recipes in this book. Although some of the ingredients may seem a bit obscure at first, once you begin to cook with them you'll quickly see the impact they have on dishes, adding saltiness, sweetness, sourness, umami, texture and pure chilli heat. Although we describe our food as non-traditional, we use Mexican ingredients extensively, so it's important to gain an understanding of these ingredients and their uses. Some of them are more difficult to get hold of than others, so wherever possible, we'll offer an easy-to-get alternative or substitute. The best place to get hold of the harder-to-find ingredients is online through specific suppliers such as Mexgrocer.co.uk or Mexgrocer.com. However, some of the larger supermarkets are now starting to stock these more specific ingredients so it's worth checking their online stores.

CHILLIES | FRESH

Jalapeño: A medium-sized chilli that has a mild to medium heat. They can be sourced through greengrocers, but the medium green chillies (normally called 'serrano') which are available in packs from most supermarkets, will suffice.

Bird's-eye chillies: These little guys pack a punch that belies their size. At the lower end of the habanero heat scale but many times hotter than a jalapeño, we use them in our Asian-inspired dishes for an authentic Eastern heat. Easy to find in most greengrocers and supermarkets.

Habanero/Scotch bonnets: Fresh habaneros are extremely hard to get hold of so we substitute these for Scotch bonnets, which are available from most greengrocers and supermarkets. They are close relations and, although slightly sweeter, still have a powerful fruity citrus heat.

CHILLIES | DRIED

Cascabel chilli: These are also known as the rattle chilli due to the noise the seeds make within the hollow stomach of the chilli. They produce a great, mild and delicate flavour that works extremely well in salsas that require more depth of flavour than intensity of heat.

Chipotle: Chipotles are smoke-dried, over-ripened jalapeños, give a mild heat and have a distinctive smoky flavour.

Dried habanero: Like chipotles, these dried chillies are normally reserved for broths and slow cooking, where we tear them in for an intense heat. Unlike the chipotles they are not smoke-dried, retaining their fruity punch. (Back in the '90s these guys were classed as the hottest chillies in the world.)

Guajillo: Large, medium-to-hot chillies that are generally used for broths but also in pastes and salsas. For salsas they are soaked, deseeded and deveined and ground into a paste.

Ancho: Ancho is the name given to a dried poblano chilli and means 'wide' in Spanish. It is a large mild chilli that we use to give added depth to broths and salsas, alongside our ancho chilli oil (see page 113).

Árbol chillies (chile de árbol): Literally meaning 'tree chilli', these are smaller but very potent chillies. We tend to use them in their dry form to add to broths or infuse in oils. As they do have similar heat and taste characteristics to cayenne pepper, you can use it instead of these chillies.

PASTES | HERBS | SPICES

Achiote paste: Also known as recado rojo, this is a red paste made from a blend of spices with the ground seeds of the annatto plant. It's mainly used as an ingredient for marinades, most famously for the classic Cochinita Pibil.

Cayenne pepper: A spicy powder derived from dried red chilli peppers, and a kitchen staple. Great for adding heat to broths and rubs.

Smoked paprika: Another kitchen staple that's easy to get hold of. It's derived from dried red chillies and differs from regular paprika in that the farmers dry the chillies over large fires, which imparts a sweet, smoky flavour to the powder.

Ground cumin: Ground cumin seeds were brought into Mexican cuisine by the Spanish many years ago. It adds an earthy, warm taste. Like most of the herbs and spices we use, this is readily available from your local supermarket.

Tinned tomatillos: Tomatillos, or Mexican husked tomatoes, are a key ingredient in fresh green salsas. A close relative of the Cape gooseberry, they are available fresh but tend to be expensive, so it's best to use the tinned variety.

Chipotle chilli powder: This adds a wonderful smoky flavour to marinades. Of course, if you're having trouble getting hold of this powder and you have dried chipotles, you can blitz them for the same effect.

Chipotles in adobo: A key ingredient in our chipotle ketchup, these are plump chipotles in a delicious, smoky adobo sauce.

Mexican oregano: You may be forgiven for thinking that this is simply 'normal' oregano but it's actually an entirely different plant, with a grassy taste and citrus note. It can be purchased through specialist suppliers, but if you're stuck you can try using dried marjoram, which has similar floral notes.

Epazote: This is a Mexican herb that has a very pungent smell and taste; think aniseed and fennel, only stronger. Its aroma has been compared to petroleum!

Star anise: A Chinese spice that we use to enhance the flavours of our meat, particularly beef. Readily available from supermarkets.

Allspice: This is the dried unripe berries of the pimenta tree ground into a powder. Mainly grown in the Caribbean, its name was coined by the English, who thought it combined the flavours of cinnamon, nutmeg and cloves.

OTHER INGREDIENTS

Onion powder: Dehydrated, ground onion.

Garlic powder: Dehydrated, ground garlic.

Salt: We always use good-quality sea salt flakes such as Maldon sea salt.

Dijon mustard: We use this as an ingredient in mayonnaise and aïoli.

Fish sauce: An Asian staple, this comes from fermenting anchovies in water and salt. We use this intense flavour mainly in our Asian-influenced recipes.

Dark soy sauce: One of the oldest condiments in the world and a kitchen staple. We tend to use dark soy as it's less salty than light soy. Perfect for adding umami to dishes.

Vinegars: We use various vinegars for a wide range of uses: aïolis and mayonnaise, pickling and adding acidity. The vinegars we use regularly are red wine vinegar, white wine vinegar, cider vinegar, sherry vinegar and muscatel vinegar.

ESSENTIAL EQUIPMENT

Cast-iron/ovenproof frying pan or griddle pan: A lot of our cooking involves roasting, braising and grilling. It's always helpful to be able to start a dish off on the hob (cooktop) and finish it in the oven, thus freeing up the hob to cook the other elements of dishes.

Blender: If there's one thing you need more than anything to cook our food, it's a blender. Most of our dishes involve some kind of paste, marinade or a blend of spices. Traditionally Mexicans would use a molcajete, a granite pestle and mortar, but for speed and efficiency, the blender is a winner.

Pestle and mortar: Essential to grind toasted spices and make salsas the traditional way.

Slow cooker: We'd highly recommend you buy one for your home kitchen. They make cooking meat over a long period of time much easier.

Tortilla press: Very useful if you want to make your own tortillas.

WHAT IS A...

TACO

The thing you've been waiting all day to eat! This is the base, the meat, the salsa, the whole shebang.

TOSTADA

Take a tortilla and deep fry it until it's crunchy.

TORTILLA

This is what we call the edible plate. Traditionally made from dried corn that has been nixtamalized and turned into a dough called masa, which is then cooked to make a tortilla. We make our tortillas from masa harina (see page 43) and they measure 12–15cm (5–6 inches). If you don't make them, corn tortillas are widely available at supermarkets and local bodegas in similar sizes.

TORTILLAS

RYE TORTILLAS

MAKES 25 TORTILLAS (AROUND 12–15CM/5–6 INCHES)

300ml (10½fl oz/1¼ cups) warm water
1 level teaspoon yeast
500g (1lb 2oz/3¼ cups) organic rye flour
2 teaspoons salt
1 tablespoon rapeseed oil
1 teaspoon sesame seeds (optional)

1. Mix the warm water with the yeast and stir. Leave until bubbles form. Then add the rye flour, salt, oil and seeds, if using, and combine to form a dough. Knead for 4 minutes, cover with a tea (dish) towel and leave for 1 hour in a warm place.

2. Follow the tortilla making process (see page 43). Repeat with the rest of the dough.

3. Cook in a hot cast-iron pan for 2 minutes on each side, or until the tortilla is slightly crunchy but still malleable.

DONG'S FLATBREADS

Dong worked for us for five years and he came in all shy and quiet. Like most shy and quiet people, he has a sparkling personality. He is also an incredible young chef. Out of the blue one day, he made these astonishing flatbreads. We normally barbecue them over coals, but you can also cook them in a frying pan or an oven.

MAKES 10–15 FLATBREADS (AROUND 30CM/12 INCHES)

3 level teaspoons dried yeast
600ml (21fl oz/2¾ cups) warm water
1kg (2lb 4oz/7½ cups) plain
   (all-purpose) flour
2 tablespoons sea salt
5 tablespoons natural yoghurt
rapeseed or garlic oil

1. Put the yeast into a bowl with the warm water and stir to dissolve, then add the flour and mix to a dough. Leave to rest for 30 minutes, then add the salt and yoghurt. Knead until incorporated, about 4–5 minutes. Leave the dough to rest in a warm place for 45 minutes. Knead again for 4–5 minutes, then set aside for 2 hours for the final rest.

2. Divide the dough into equal portions and roll out to a 5mm (¼ inch) thickness. Heat a cast-iron pan or griddle to high, add a slick of rapeseed or garlic oil and cook the breads one at a time for about 2 minutes each side.

CORN TORTILLAS

A taco press makes life much simpler. You can use shop-bought corn tortillas for our recipes if you don't fancy making your own.

MAKES 25 TORTILLAS (AROUND 12–15CM/5–6 INCHES)

*160g (5½oz/scant 1¼ cups) masa harina
(or blue masa harina for blue tortillas)
½ teaspoon salt
100ml (3½fl oz/scant ½ cup) hot water
1 tablespoon rapeseed oil or melted lard*

1. Mix the masa harina and salt in a bowl and stir in the water slowly while mixing the dough with your hand. Add the oil or lard and knead to form a smooth dough. If the dough is too wet, add some more masa harina and if it feels flaky and dry, add some more water. Leave to rest at room temperature for a minimum of 30 minutes.

2. Next, divide the dough up into 25 equal-sized balls.

3. Cut a freezer bag in half to create two square sections and place onto a hard surface or on the bottom of your tortilla press. Add a ball of masa, then place the other freezer bag square over the top of the dough. Either push your hand down firmly on the dough or use a rolling pin to create a 12–15cm (5–6-inch) circular tortilla, or if you are using a taco press, press down using the crank lever. Remove the plastic squares and set the tortilla aside. Repeat, separating each pressed tortilla with a square of baking (parchment) paper.

4. Heat a heavy-based pan and add the tortillas – cook for 1 minute on each side, or until they soufflé slightly. Remove after a minute or two and wrap in a tea (dish) towel to keep warm.

ACOS

PORTER BRAISED BEEF SHORT-RIB & BURNT SPRING ONION CREMA

INGREDIENTS

SERVES 4

2kg (4lb 8oz) beef short-ribs
1½ tablespoons sea salt
2 tablespoons olive oil
1 onion, finely chopped
1 leek, roughly chopped
7 garlic cloves, finely chopped
70ml (2½fl oz/scant ⅓ cup) soy sauce
70ml (2½fl oz/⅔ cup) ketchup
130g (4½oz/½ cup) brown sugar
3 star anise
1 tablespoon cayenne pepper
2 tablespoons chile de árbol powder
4 dried chipotle chillies
5 dried porcini mushrooms
1 x 440ml (15fl oz/scant 2 cups)
*   can of porter, or other dark beer*

To serve:

8 corn tortillas (see page 43)
100ml (3½fl oz/scant ½ cup) burnt
*   spring onion crema (see page 113)*
4 tablespoons chopped coriander
*   (cilantro)*
chilli flakes, to serve
2 limes, quartered
4 tablespoons pico de gallo
*   (see page 109)*

1. Sprinkle the short-ribs with the salt and set aside for 2 hours.

2. Heat 1 tablespoon of the oil in a frying pan on a medium heat and add the short ribs. You want to sear the ribs on all sides and get a deep-brown, caramel colour on them. Don't skip this step, as it's imperative for building the umami flavour. When browned, remove from the heat.

3. In an ovenproof casserole, heat the remaining tablespoon of oil on a medium heat and add the onion and leek. Cook for 5 minutes, then add the garlic. After 3 minutes, add the soy sauce, ketchup, brown sugar, anise, cayenne pepper, chile de árbol, chipotles, mushrooms and beer. Cook the mixture for 30 minutes, uncovered, on a low heat, then add the short ribs to the pot. If there seems to be too little liquid to cover the ribs, add some water.

Continued...

4. Preheat your oven to 130°C (250°F/ Gas ½). Once it's up to temperature, cover the casserole with a lid, then transfer to the oven and cook for 6–8 hours. The short-ribs are ready when you can scoop some meat off them with a teaspoon. Remove from the oven and, when cool, take the ribs out and put them on a tray. Put the casserole back on a medium heat and reduce the sauce for another 20 minutes or so – this will be your glaze, so you're looking for a sauce that will thickly coat the back of a spoon.

5. When you're ready to eat, heat a frying pan over a medium heat and add the ribs, rib side down. Using a brush, glaze the ribs with the reduced sauce, then flip them and cook them meat side down for 5 minutes. Turn and brush again.

6. Warm the tortillas in a dry pan. Place two on each plate and cover the tacos with a thin layer of the burnt spring onion crema. Pull the meat away from the bone of each rib, using a fork and spoon, and place on the tacos. Sprinkle the coriander over, followed by some chilli flakes. Serve with the lime and pico de gallo on the side.

BONE-IN RIB-EYE, TOMATOES, BURNT SPRING ONIONS & SHACK SALSA

INGREDIENTS

SERVES 4

2 x 400g (14oz) bone-in rib-eye steaks
3 tablespoons butter
4 garlic cloves, peeled
1 sprig of thyme
sea salt and freshly ground black pepper
100ml (3½fl oz/scant ½ cup) red wine
4 large Datterini tomatoes, or any very
    sweet tomatoes
extra-virgin olive oil
1 red onion, finely sliced into rings
    and soaked in cold water
thyme oil (see below)
1 tablespoon ancho chilli oil (see page 113)
2 tablespoons shack salsa verde, plus
    3 tablespoons to serve (see page 118)
a handful of coriander (cilantro), chopped
1 teaspoon ground red chilli powder
a bunch of burnt spring onions
    (see page 113)
10 corn tortillas (see page 43)

For the thyme oil:
4 sprigs thyme, washed and dried
200ml (7fl oz/scant 1 cup) extra-virgin olive
    or rapeseed oil
peel of ½ lemon

Ask your butcher for bone-in rib-eye steaks that have been dry-aged for at least 28 days. The steak will taste best when cooked over charcoal, but a heavy-based frying pan and intense heat will do the trick. Be sure to take the steaks out of the fridge at least an hour before you intend to cook them, so they are at room temperature. The thyme oil makes more than you'll need. Keep it in a sterilized jar and use it for salads, marinades and dressings.

1. To make the thyme oil, bruise the herbs by whacking them on a table a few times. Then heat the olive oil and thyme in a saucepan until small bubbles form on the surface of the oil. Allow to cool, add the lemon peel and transfer to a sterilized jar.

2. When you're ready to cook the tacos, turn your hob to high and place your frying pan or griddle on to get it seriously hot (leave it for at least 5 minutes). Pat dry the steaks (this is important so that the steaks char rather than steam) and put them into the pan. Keep them moving around in the pan and, after 3–4 minutes, flip them over.

Continued...

3. Add 1 tablespoon of the butter to the pan and baste the steak with the rendered fat and melted butter. Add the garlic and thyme. Add a big pinch of the sea salt and pepper to the side of the rib-eye that's been cooking, cook for a further 4 minutes (for medium rare), then transfer the steaks to a warm plate. Add ½ tablespoon of the remaining butter on top of each steak and leave to rest for at least 5 minutes.

4. Add the red wine to the pan with the remaining butter. Turn up the heat and let the sauce reduce for 5 minutes, then set aside.

5. Cut the tomatoes into 1cm (½ inch) slices, then drizzle on some olive oil and sprinkle with sea salt and pepper. Place the sliced tomatoes on a serving plate and add the drained red onions. Slice the steak across the grain at a 45-degree angle into 3cm (1¼ inch) segments and place on top of the tomatoes. Drizzle with a little thyme oil, the ancho chilli oil, 2 tablespoons of salsa verde, and sprinkle with the coriander, red chilli and some sea salt. Place the burnt spring onions on the side.

6. Warm the tortillas in a dry frying pan, then serve, with each guest grabbing a couple of slices of steak and some tomatoes and onions, and the extra salsa verde. If you like it hot, have some habanero hot sauce on the side.

CARNE ASADA & CHIPOTLE CASHEW NUT SALSA

INGREDIENTS

SERVES 4

500g (1lb 2oz) bavette, onglet steak or rump

For the marinade:
300ml (10½fl oz/1¼ cups) smoky steak marinade (see page 108)

To serve:
16 corn tortillas (see page 43)
4 tablespoons chipotle cashew nut salsa (see page 108)
4 tablespoons pico de gallo (see page 109)
2 limes, quartered
100ml (3½fl oz/scant ½ cup) sour cream or crema (see page 109)
a handful of coriander leaves (cilantro)

This is my take on a classic Mexican street food taco. Throughout Mexico, these vary in both recipe and presentation, so I thought we'd do the same with our breddos Tacos version. I use the chipotle cashew nut salsa to add a creamy, nutty and smoky flavour to the taco. Purists would definitely frown at our treatment of the carne asada, but the taste combination speaks for itself.

1. Rub the smoky steak marinade all over the steak and leave the meat to marinate in the refrigerator, covered, for at least an hour and up to 2 days.

2. When you're ready, get the grill or pan as hot as you can, about 5 minutes on a high heat, then add the steak and cook until it's charred on the outside and medium rare on the inside, about 3 minutes on each side. Take the steak off the grill and let it rest for 5 minutes in a warm place. In the meantime, warm up the tortillas in a dry frying pan and wrap them in a clean tea (dish) towel to keep them warm.

3. Slice the steak against the grain into 2cm (¾ inch) thick slices. Put a few slices of steak on each tortilla, add some cashew nut salsa, some pico de gallo, a squirt of lime, a spoonful of sour cream or crema, and some coriander to garnish.

BEEF TARTARE, TOMATILLO & JALAPENO

INGREDIENTS

SERVES 4 AS A SNACK OR
2 AS A MAIN COURSE

150g (5½oz) good-quality beef fillet
1 shallot
3 cornichons
1 long red chilli
1 jalapeño chilli
1 tomatillo, dry roasted
*1 garlic clove, sliced wafer thin and
    sautéed in olive oil until crispy*
1 teaspoon olive oil
1 tablespoon red wine vinegar
sea salt and freshly ground black pepper
1 teaspoon Dijon mustard
2 tablespoons extra-virgin olive oil
4 tostadas (see page 40)
4 quail egg yolks
*4 tablespoons finely chopped coriander
    (cilantro), to garnish*
thinly sliced radishes, to garnish
*1 tablespoon breddos hot sauce
    (see page 110) or to taste*
edible flowers (optional), to garnish

1. Put the beef fillet into the freezer to firm up for 30 minutes. Very finely dice the shallot and leave to soak in a bowl of cold water while the beef is in the freezer.

2. Finely dice the cornichons, red chilli, jalapeño, and finely chop the tomatillo and crispy garlic and put them into a bowl with the drained shallots. Slice the beef fillet and cut into 5mm (¼ inch) cubes, add to the bowl with the teaspoon of olive oil and mix together.

3. Add the red wine vinegar, a pinch of salt, a bigger pinch of pepper, the mustard and the extra-virgin olive oil and mix. Place a tostada (or 2) on each plate and add a spoonful of tartare mix. Spread out to cover the surface. Place a raw egg yolk in the middle and sprinkle with salt and pepper.

4. Garnish with the coriander, radish slices and breddos hot sauce, and finish with edible flowers, if using.

SUNDAY SHORT-RIB BARBACOA NACHOS

INGREDIENTS

SERVES 2 AS A MAIN MEAL OR 4 AS A SNACK

200g (7oz) braised meat (short-rib, brisket, barbacoa etc.)
1 x 200g (7oz) bag of salted corn tortilla chips
100ml (3½fl oz/scant ½ cup) sour cream
250g (9oz) mature Cheddar cheese, grated
100g (3½oz/½ cup) refried beans (see page 110)
100g (3½oz/½ cup) guacamole (see page 111)
100g (3½oz/scant ½ cup) pico de gallo (see page 109)
juice of 1 lime
coriander (cilantro), to garnish

These are the ultimate Sunday comfort food, and are a great way of using up some short-rib (see page 46) or barbacoa (see page 78) that you have left over. The recipe below is a guide – feel free to raid your fridge and use up whatever you might have left. Quite often the best Sunday nachos I've had were created through total lack of direction. This recipe is all about layering your ingredients. Unlike most other nachos, we like to design ours like a lasagne, using the chips as lasagne sheets, the meat and beans as the ragù and the cheese as the béchamel. The results are exactly what you want on a lazy Sunday night.

1. Preheat the oven to 180°C (350°F/ Gas 4). Line the bottom of a large ovenproof pan or dish with some of the meat mixture, then layer some chips over the top, then add some sour cream and Cheddar. Repeat the meat, chips, sour cream, cheese process until you get almost to the top of your pan or dish (make sure you have a little sour cream and cheese left over). Add the refried beans layer, then even more cheese.

2. Put into the oven for 20 minutes, then take out and add a layer of guacamole, followed by the pico de gallo, then more sour cream.

3. Squeeze the lime juice over the top and garnish with coriander. Serve with a spoon.

YUCATAN-STYLE CHICKEN & MANGO HABANERO SALSA

INGREDIENTS

SERVES 4

For the marinade:
1 tablespoon cayenne pepper
1 tablespoon smoked paprika
1 teaspoon dried oregano
1 tablespoon sea salt
1 tablespoon freshly ground black pepper
4 tablespoons orange juice
2 tablespoons allspice
4 tablespoons pineapple juice
2 tablespoons lime juice
2 habanero chillies, stems removed
2 jalapeño chillies, stems removed
3 tablespoons rapeseed oil

For the chicken:
5 boneless chicken thighs, skin on
olive oil, for frying
juice of 1 lime

For the tacos:
12 corn tortillas (see page 43)
4 tablespoons mango, lime & habanero
    salsa (see page 111)
4 tablespoons coriander (cilantro)
pickled habaneros (see page 112), to taste
4 tablespoons crema (see page 109)
    or sour cream
4 limes, quartered

1. Mix the marinade ingredients together in the jug of your blender, then pulse until you have a smooth paste. Score the chicken thighs and rub the marinade into them. Place in a non-reactive container, cover and leave to marinate for at least 6 hours in a refrigerator.

2. Fire up your hob and put your ovenproof pan or griddle on to heat up with a slick of oil. Preheat your oven to 200°C (400°F/Gas 6).

3. Put the chicken thighs on the griddle, skin side down, and cook for 6–7 minutes, occasionally moving them to ensure they don't stick. Flip them over, cover the griddle or pan with foil and place in the oven for 20 minutes or until they're cooked through, then take the cover off the pan and put back into the oven for another 10 minutes. Take the chicken out and leave to rest. Meanwhile warm up your tortillas in a dry pan.

4. When the chicken has cooled a little, take two forks to it and shred it into a bowl. Sprinkle with the lime juice.

5. To assemble your tacos, take a tortilla and put in a big pinch of chicken, a teaspoon of mango, lime & habanero salsa, a pinch of coriander, a couple of pickled habaneros, a teaspoon of crema on top, and a squeeze of lime.

CRISPY CHICKEN SKIN TOSTADAS WITH AVOCADO & ANCHO CHILLI OIL

INGREDIENTS

SERVES 4 AS A SNACK

1 tablespoon rapeseed oil
skin from 4 chicken thighs
1 teaspoon flaky sea salt
8 tablespoons avocado mojo
   (see page 112)
4 teaspoons ancho chilli oil
   (see page 113)

1. Heat a frying pan over a medium heat and add the rapeseed oil. Put the chicken skin in, fat side down, and sprinkle the salt evenly over. Turn the temperature down and cook slowly for 7 minutes, or until the fat has rendered down and you're left with crispy chicken skin. Turn the skin over and repeat the process. Once the skin is done, remove and leave to drain on kitchen paper for 1 minute.

2. Take the skin, which should be flat and crispy, and break each thigh piece in half. Place 2 pieces of skin on each plate and spoon over some avocado mojo. Drizzle over some ancho chilli oil and serve.

TRIPLE-COOKED HABANERO CHICKEN WINGS

INGREDIENTS

SERVES 4

1kg (2lb 4oz) chicken wings, split into two
    (ask your butcher to remove any hair
    and the tip)
sea salt
500ml (18fl oz/2 cups) rapeseed oil,
    for frying
cascabel chilli salt (see page 117), to taste
freshly ground black pepper
100g (3½oz) Stilton or other blue cheese
150g (5½oz/scant ¾ cup) mayonnaise
habanero or Scotch bonnet salsa
    (see page 119), to taste
8 corn tortillas (see page 43)
2 limes, quartered
a handful of coriander (cilantro),
    finely chopped
½ head of celery, peeled and
    cut into 5mm (¼ inch) fingers,
    kept in ice-cold water

*You'll need an oil-safe temperature
thermometer for this recipe; they're worth
investing in, as they help ensure that your
food is cooked to the correct temperature.
If the habanero sauce is too hot, feel free
to replace it with the avocado mojo on
page 112.*

1. Season the chicken wings with a pinch
of sea salt.

2. Heat the rapeseed oil in a deep pan or
pot to 120°C (245°F). Add the wings and
fry for 5 minutes, then remove them from
the oil and leave them to drain on kitchen
paper. Place in the freezer for a minimum
of 3 hours. Then take the wings out of the
freezer and fry again at 120°C (245°F) for
4 minutes. Repeat the draining process
and freeze again for 4 hours. (The wings
can now be stored frozen until you're
ready to use them.)

3. When you're ready to serve, reheat
the oil to 190°C (375°F). Add the frozen
chicken wings and fry for 4 minutes, then
drain and season with cascabel chilli salt
and black pepper. Mix the Stilton and
mayonnaise together to make the blue
cheese dip.

4. Spoon the habanero salsa onto a tortilla
and place the wings on top. Serve with the
lime quarters, coriander and celery sticks.

TRIPLE-STACKED CLUB TOSTADAS WITH CHICKEN & BACON

INGREDIENTS

SERVES 4

4 x 50g (2oz) cooked chicken breasts
olive oil, for frying
8 rashers (slices) smoked bacon
8 tostadas (see page 40)
2 tablespoons mayonnaise
200g (7oz/1 cup) refried beans
    (see page 110)
1 head cos lettuce, shredded
pico de gallo (see page 109), to taste
breddos hot sauce (see page 110), to taste
sea salt and freshly ground black pepper
250g (9oz) mature Cheddar cheese,
    grated

This is a comfort-food tostada that's great to make when you have a bunch of ingredients that need using up in your fridge.

1. Preheat your oven to 200°C (400°F/ Gas 6). Shred the chicken with your hands into 4–5cm (1½–2 inch) pieces. Heat a frying pan, add a slick of olive oil and cook the chicken for 4–5 minutes. Set the chicken aside, then add the bacon rashers to the pan and cook until crispy, 3–4 minutes on each side.

2. Assemble your clubs on an ovenproof tray, starting with a tostada, followed by a spoonful of mayonnaise smeared over the surface, then refried beans, then some lettuce, chicken, bacon and pico de gallo. Season with salt and pepper. Now on top of this, add another tostada and repeat the process with the remaining fillings. Cover the top with breddos hot sauce.

3. Put a mound of cheese on top, to cover the sauce, to complete the triple stack, and place in the oven for 5 minutes, or until melted. Serve on plates.

DUCK CARNITAS, GEM LETTUCE, PLUMS & PICKLES

INGREDIENTS

SERVES 4

4 duck legs
3 teaspoons sea salt
1 teaspoon black pepper
1 onion, quartered
2 dried chipotle chillies
8 dried plums (use apricots if you
   can't find plums)
1 head of garlic
1 tablespoon whole black peppercorns
2 whole star anise
200g (7oz/scant 1 cup) duck fat
4 baby gem lettuces
white sesame seeds, to garnish
2 limes, quartered, to serve

For the pink pickled onions:
1 red onion, thinly sliced
2 large habanero chillies, deseeded,
   veined and thinly sliced
100ml (3½fl oz/scant ½ cup) freshly
   squeezed, strained lime juice

This is an awesome dish to serve up at dinner parties or get-togethers as a canapé. By using baby gem lettuce as the tortilla (the Koreans call it Ssam), it feels light and healthy, but it always delivers on flavour. The best thing about this recipe is that you can use any leftover duck for grilled cheese sandwiches, nachos and salads.

1. Cover the duck with the salt and pepper and leave overnight, covered, in the fridge.

2. The next day, preheat the oven to 160°C (300°F/Gas 2). Put the legs fat (skin) side down into an ovenproof frying pan and cook on medium heat for about 15 minutes. You're looking to render the fat from the legs and release their juices. Turn the legs over and add the onion, chipotles, dried plums, garlic, peppercorns, anise and duck fat. Cover the pan with foil and put into the oven for 2–2½ hours.

3. Take the foil off the pan and increase the oven temperature to 200°C (400°F/Gas 6). Cook the duck for a further 15 minutes, then take out of the oven and set aside to rest.

Continued...

4. Prepare the pink pickled onions by macerating the sliced red onion and habanero in the lime juice. Set aside in the fridge.

5. In the meantime, prepare the baby gems by snipping off the roots and separating the leaves of the lettuce with your hands – you'll find they have a natural boat shape, perfect for filling with food.

6. Shred the meat off the duck legs, making sure to mash the garlic and chipotle into the cooking sauce and incorporating it into the meat. Fill each lettuce cup with a generous helping of duck, followed by a plum from the cooking sauce, some prepared pink pickled onions, sesame seeds and a squirt of lime.

BUTTERMILK-FRIED CHICKEN, PICO DE GALLO & HABANERO AIOLI

INGREDIENTS

SERVES 4

For the chicken:
250ml (9fl oz/1 cup) buttermilk
1 tablespoon sea salt
8 boneless chicken thighs,
   cut lengthways in half

For the seasoned flour mix:
200g (7oz/1½ cups) plain
   (all-purpose) flour
200g (7oz/3 cups) panko breadcrumbs
   or good-quality breadcrumbs
1 tablespoon smoked paprika
1 tablespoon cayenne pepper
1 tablespoon chipotle powder (optional)
1 teaspoon allspice
1 teaspoon garlic powder
1 teaspoon onion powder
1 teaspoon Colman's mustard powder
1 teaspoon baking powder
500ml (18fl oz/2 cups) rapeseed oil

For the tacos:
16 corn tortillas (see page 43)
6 tablespoons habanero aïoli
   (see page 114)
6 tablespoons pico de gallo
   (see page 109)

1. Mix together the buttermilk and salt, then add the chicken thighs and leave to soak for 24 hours in the refrigerator.

2. The next day, combine the flour, panko, paprika, cayenne, chipotle (if using), allspice, garlic powder, onion powder, mustard powder and baking powder in a large bowl. Take the chicken out of the buttermilk and plunge it into the flour mix, making sure you pack the flour on with your hands so it sticks – it's messy, but it's worth it for the crunch. Leave the chicken on a wire rack for 10 minutes.

3. In the meantime, heat the oil in a deep pan or pot until it reaches 180°C (355°F) or the point when a small amount of flour sizzles when added to the oil. Add a few chicken pieces at a time and cook for 4–5 minutes, or until a probe registers 75°C (165°F) in the thickest part of the chicken. Leave the chicken on a rack to cool and drain.

4. Warm up your tortillas in a dry frying pan, smear them with some habanero aïoli, then place the chicken on top with a spoonful of pico de gallo and some more aïoli.

JERK QUAIL, MANGO LIME & HABANERO SALSA

INGREDIENTS

SERVES 4

4 quails
olive oil
4 tablespoons mango, lime
   & habanero salsa (see page 111)
8 corn tortillas (see page 43)
bunch of burnt spring onions
   (see page 113)

For the jerk marinade:
1 tablespoon allspice berries
1 tablespoon black peppercorns
½ teaspoon ground cinnamon
½ teaspoon freshly grated nutmeg
¼ bunch of thyme, leaves picked
5 spring onions (scallions),
   roughly chopped
3 garlic cloves, roughly chopped
2 Scotch bonnet chillies,
   roughly chopped
1 tablespoon dark brown sugar
2 tablespoons dark soy sauce
juice of 2 limes
sea salt

For the jerk glaze:
125ml (4fl oz/½ cup) honey
125g (4oz/generous ½ cup) sugar
3 garlic cloves, crushed
1 teaspoon jerk marinade (see above)

1. Crush the allspice and peppercorns and blitz to a paste with the rest of the marinade ingredients. Set aside a teaspoon of the paste for the jerk glaze, then rub the rest of the paste into the quails and marinate for 4 hours, or overnight in the refrigerator.

2. To make the jerk glaze, combine the honey and sugar in a pan and cook until it has the consistency of syrup. Add the garlic and the jerk marinade and remove from the heat.

3. When you're ready to cook, preheat your oven to 200°C (400°F/Gas 6). Heat a slick of olive oil in an ovenproof frying pan, add the quails and sear until browned on all sides, about 5 minutes. Brush the quails with some of the glaze and continue to cook for another 3 minutes, then place in the oven to finish for 5 minutes.

4. When you're ready to serve, arrange the quails on a serving board and loosely drizzle some more glaze on them, followed by 1 tablespoon of the mango salsa per bird. Serve with tortillas and burnt spring onions.

GUINEA FOWL
WITH AVOCADO

INGREDIENTS

SERVES 4

1 guinea fowl, giblets removed
rapeseed oil
sea salt and freshly ground black pepper
1 tablespoon ground cumin
1 dried habanero chilli, finely chopped
1 guajillo or ancho chilli, finely chopped

For the guinea fowl with guinea fowl tea:
olive oil
1 carrot, finely diced
1 onion, finely diced
1 celery stalk, finely diced
200ml (7fl oz/scant 1 cup) chicken stock
1 bay leaf
1 sprig of thyme
1 tablespoon black peppercorns
120ml (4fl oz/½ cup) red wine

To serve:
8 corn tortillas (see page 43)
1 avocado, finely sliced
1 teaspoon chipotle powder
1 lime, quartered

1. Preheat your oven to 180°C (350°F/ Gas 4).

2. Rub the guinea fowl with some oil, then sprinkle with salt, pepper and the spices. Place in a roasting tray and cook in the oven for 1 hour. When it's cooked (when the juices from the thigh run clear when pierced with a skewer), remove from the oven and let cool for 10 minutes.

3. Warm the tortillas in a dry frying pan and add a carved slice of guinea fowl per tortilla. Top with the avocado, a dusting of chipotle powder and a squeeze of lime.

OPTIONAL: GUINEA FOWL WITH GUINEA FOWL TEA

1. Once the guinea fowl has cooled, pull the meat off the carcass and set aside. Put the carcass into a stockpot with some oil and brown for 5 minutes. Add the carrot, onion and celery and cook for 5 minutes. Add the stock, bay leaf, thyme and peppercorns and cook on a medium heat until reduced by half, about 20 minutes. Add the wine and reduce until you have a velvety sauce. Strain the sauce through a fine mesh sieve into another pan. Set aside.

2. When you're ready to serve, place the meat in a saucepan with a tablespoon of sauce. Heat for 3 minutes, then set aside.

3. Fill a shot glass or egg cup with the sauce and serve as a beverage alongside. Then follow step 3 above to make the taco.

COCHINITA PORK PIBIL, X NI PEK & SOUR ORANGE

INGREDIENTS

SERVES 4

*1 kg (2lb 4oz) boneless neck end pork
shoulder, brined overnight in 10%
salt-water brine (optional; see step 1)*
sea salt
*500ml (18fl oz/2 cups) sour orange juice,
or half normal orange juice and half
grapefruit juice*
200g (7oz/scant 1 cup) achiote paste
10 garlic cloves
*100g (3½oz/½ cup) guajillo chillies,
deseeded, deveined, and soaked in
warm water for 10 minutes*
*2 cloves, toasted and crushed in a pestle
and mortar*
1 small white onion, roughly chopped
1 large defrosted banana leaf (optional)
12 corn tortillas (see page 43)
6 tablespoons x ni pek (see page 116)
chopped coriander (cilantro), to garnish
1 lime, quartered

1. If you're brining the pork, first create a 10% salt water brine by dissolving 100g (3½oz/½ cup) of salt per 1 litre (1¾ pints/4 cups) of water as needed to cover the pork. Submerge the pork and brine overnight. Alternatively, if you don't have time, simply rub the meat with sea salt and allow to sit for 30 minutes.

2. Place the orange juice, achiote paste, garlic, guajillo, cloves and onion in a blender and blitz to a paste. Rub the paste over the pork and leave to marinate overnight in the refrigerator.

3. Preheat the oven to 160°C (300°F/ Gas 2). Wrap the pork in the banana leaf or some baking (parchment) paper. Place in a deep casserole dish and cover with foil twice to ensure no steam escapes. Cover with a lid and cook for around 2½–3 hours, or until meltingly tender. Remove the banana leaf or parchment and shred the pork, then gently stir together with all of the cooking juices.

4. Toast the tortillas in a dry pan, then scoop a little of the pork pibil into the centre of each one and garnish with the x ni pek, and finally some chopped coriander and lime wedges.

PORK BELLY, BLACK PUDDING, TOMATILLO SALSA & CRACKLING

INGREDIENTS

SERVES 4

100g (3½oz) flaky sea salt, plus extra
1 tablespoon smoked paprika
1 tablespoon fennel seeds
1 tablespoon coriander seeds
1 tablespoon ground cloves
400g (14oz) boneless pork belly, skin on
*   and scored (ask your butcher to do this)*
1.5 litres (2½ pints/6 cups) chicken stock
250g (9oz) black pudding (blood sausage),
*   thinly sliced*

To serve:

8 corn tortillas (see page 43)
50g (1¾oz/¼ cup) tomatillo salsa
*   (see page 115)*
1 tablespoon breddos hot sauce
*   (see page 110)*
a handful of coriander (cilantro)
*   leaves (optional)*

1. Mix the salt and spices together and spread them over the meat side of the belly. Refrigerate for 24 hours.

2. When you're ready to cook, preheat the oven to 240°C (475°F/Gas 9). Rinse the belly and pat dry. Heavily rub the skin with salt, then place the belly in an ovenproof dish or roasting tray into which it will fit snugly, skin side up. Pour in the chicken stock, being careful not to get the skin wet (it needs to be dry to form the crackling). Cook the belly for 20–30 minutes, or until the skin blisters and crackles. Turn the temperature down to 150°C (300°F/Gas 2) and cook the belly for 3½ hours, or until tender. Once done, remove the pork and set aside to cool. Once cool, cut the belly into strips 10cm (4 inches) long and 4cm (1½ inches) wide and set aside.

3. Heat a frying pan over a medium heat and add the black pudding. Fry until soft, but still malleable, for about 1 minute. Remove and set aside.

4. In the same pan, warm up the tortillas – once they are puffing up, place on your serving dish or plates. On each tortilla place a couple of slices of black pudding, a slice of pork belly and a drizzle of tomatillo salsa and breddos hot sauce. Garnish with coriander, if using, and serve.

PORK RIBS WITH PICKLED WATERMELON

INGREDIENTS

SERVES 4

For the pork:
1 tablespoon rapeseed oil
1 onion, chopped
1 carrot, chopped
1 celery stalk, chopped
2kg (4lb 8oz) pork belly ribs
1 bottle of Corona or Dos Equis beer
1 teaspoon allspice
1 head of garlic, separated into cloves
2 tablespoons agave syrup or honey
2 teaspoons cayenne pepper
1 tablespoon brown sugar
1 tablespoon sea salt
1 tablespoon freshly ground black pepper
8 corn tortillas (see page 43)

For the watermelon:
100ml (3½fl oz/scant ½ cup) cider vinegar
2 long red chillies, finely sliced
a pinch of sea salt and freshly ground
    black pepper
1 tablespoon agave syrup
1 teaspoon coriander seeds
½ watermelon, cut into 3cm (1¼ inch)
    cubes (rind removed and also cut
    into 3cm/1¼ inch chunks)

These ribs are great for when you have a barbecue or big gathering planned.

1. Preheat your oven to 150°C (300°F/Gas 2).

2. Place a roasting tray over a medium heat. Add the oil and, when hot, add the onion. Cook for 5 minutes, stirring occasionally, then add the carrot and celery. Add the pork belly ribs and the beer, allspice, garlic, agave, cayenne, brown sugar, salt and pepper. Bring to the boil, then cover tightly with foil and place in the oven for 4 hours.

3. In the meantime, pickle the watermelon. Place the vinegar, chillies, salt, pepper, agave and coriander seeds in a saucepan, bring to the boil then remove from the heat and immediately pour over the watermelon cubes. Set aside for at least 1 hour to pickle.

4. After 4 hours, the pork should be fork-tender; take the foil off the tray and turn the oven up to 200°C (400°F/Gas 6) for 10 minutes. Carefully remove the ribs and place on a serving tray, then put the roasting tray over a medium heat and boil to reduce the sauce by a third.

5. Pour the sauce over the ribs or into a bowl. Scatter the watermelon over the pork. Serve with warm tortillas.

MUTTON BARBACOA WITH PEA MOLE

INGREDIENTS

SERVES 6

½ mutton shoulder, about 1kg (2lb 4oz)

For the marinade:
1 teaspoon cumin seeds
1 teaspoon Mexican oregano
1 tablespoon ancho powder
1 tablespoon cayenne pepper
1 teaspoon chile de árbol
a big handful of chipotle powder
20 garlic cloves, peeled
a big handful of sea salt and freshly
    ground black pepper
100ml (3½fl oz/scant ½ cup) rapeseed oil

For the pea mole:
150g (1¼ cups) frozen peas
50g (1¾oz/⅓ cup) sesame seeds
50g (1¾oz/½ cup) skinned almonds
3 tablespoons pumpkin seeds
juice of 2 limes
handful of mint leaves, finely chopped
½ teaspoon chilli flakes
½ teaspoon each of salt and pepper
1 garlic clove, finely chopped

To serve:
18 corn tortillas (page 43)
9 tablespoons pea mole (see above)
6 tablespoons sour cream
6 tablespoons pico de gallo (see page 109)
6 tablespoons habanero salsa (page 119)
4 tablespoons chopped coriander (cilantro)
1 lime, quartered
pickled habaneros (see page 112), to taste

This recipe works fantastically in a smoker – if you have one – but it works just as well in the oven.

1. Put the ingredients for the marinade into a blender and blitz on high speed, scraping down the sides of the jug after a couple of minutes to ensure everything is evenly mixed. Rub the marinade all over the mutton shoulder and leave to marinate in the fridge for at least 24 hours.

2. Take your mutton out of the fridge at least 1 hour before you cook it, and preheat your smoker or oven to 110°C (225°F/Gas ¼). Put the mutton into a tray, wrapped in banana leaves or baking (parchment) paper, cover it twice with foil, and put into the oven for 8 hours. Check the tenderness – it may need another couple of hours. When you're happy, take the mutton out and let it rest for at least 30 minutes, then shred with two forks.

3. In the meantime, make the pea mole. Cook the peas in boiling water for 2 minutes, then transfer to a bowl of ice-cold water. Toast the sesame seeds, almonds and pumpkin seeds in a dry frying pan for 2 minutes. Then put the seeds, drained peas and remaining ingredients in a blender and pulse for 1 minute, until you have a smooth, velvety sauce.

4. Warm up your tortillas. Spoon some mole on each taco, followed by the shredded mutton, sour cream, salsas, coriander, lime juice and pickled habanero.

PRESA IBERICA, ROASTED MARCONA ALMONDS & SALTED CHILLI PASTE

INGREDIENTS

SERVES 4

500g (1lb 2oz) presa ibérica
1 tablespoon rapeseed oil
sea salt
3 garlic cloves, crushed
1 teaspoon butter
4 tablespoons veal stock or beef stock, plus
    extra if needed

To serve:
8 tostadas (see page 40)
a handful of mustard greens, blanched
    in boiling water for 2 minutes and
    cooled in ice-cold water
salted chilli paste (see page 115), to taste
100g (3½oz/¾ cup) Marcona almonds,
    roasted in a dry pan for 5 minutes and
    split in half
1 teaspoon extra-virgin olive oil
a handful of coriander (cilantro) sprigs

Ibérico pigs roam free for a large part of their lives, feeding on acorns that have fallen from oak trees in dehesas (pastures). This diet, combined with the natural exercise they get from being free to move wherever they wish, creates a truly unique flavour profile. If you have never tried Ibérico ham, find your nearest Spanish retailer and buy some immediately. Its flavour is astonishing. The presa cut comes from the end of the loin of the pig, next to the neck. Unlike most pork dishes, you want to serve it medium rare – due to the nature of the pig and the life it leads, this is totally safe.

1. Put a cast-iron frying pan on a medium heat. Rub the presa ibérica with a thin layer of oil and salt. When the pan is hot, add the presa and the garlic. Cook for 3–4 minutes, then flip. Cook for another 3 minutes, basting with any juices that have run out of the meat. If you have a temperature probe, you need to test the meat after about 5 minutes of cooking – when it reaches around 55°C (130°F), take it off the heat and let it rest for 3–4 minutes. If you don't have a probe, hold your thumb to your middle finger and feel the area underneath your thumb – if the presa feels this tender, it's medium rare.

Continued...

2. Remove the pork to a board and add the butter and 4 tablespoons of the veal stock to the pan. Cook for a further 3 minutes. If the stock reduces too much, add a little extra to the pan.

3. To assemble the dish, place 2 tostadas on each plate, followed by the mustard greens and a teaspoon of the salted chilli paste. Slice the presa at an angle into 5mm (¼ inch) slices and place on top of the mustard greens. Sprinkle the toasted almonds over, with a drizzle of olive oil, a spoonful of the reduced veal stock from the pan and a scattering of coriander.

GREEN CHORIZO & DUCK EGG

INGREDIENTS

SERVES 4

6 serrano or jalapeño chillies
6 garlic cloves, unpeeled
1 large bunch of coriander (cilantro),
*   plus a handful of leaves, to serve*
1 large bunch of flat-leaf parsley
60ml (2fl oz/¼ cup) Moscatel vinegar
2kg (4lb 8oz) coarsely ground pork
*   shoulder (ask your butcher to do*
*   this for you)*
2 tablespoons sea salt
2 cloves
1 dried bay leaf
1 teaspoon dried Mexican oregano
¼ teaspoon ground cumin
1 teaspoon ground coriander
½ teaspoon freshly ground black pepper
rapeseed oil
4 duck eggs or large regular eggs
8 tostadas (see page 40)
4 teaspoons crumbled queso fresco
*   or feta cheese*
breddos hot sauce, to taste (see page 110)
1 lemon, quartered

People normally think of chorizo as being red, but in Mexico they make the most incredible, vibrant, green chorizo that tastes so much fresher, herbier and lighter than the red version. This is a great dish to eat at any time of day, not least the morning after a night of overindulgence, should you have some to hand.

1. Heat a large frying pan over a medium heat. Put in the chillies and garlic cloves and cook, turning from time to time. Both the chillies and garlic should be soft and blackened in spots. Remove from the heat and allow the garlic cloves to cool, then peel them.

2. Pick all the leaves off of the coriander and parsley. Place the leaves in a blender along with the cooked chillies and garlic and the vinegar, and purée until smooth.

3. Place the pork in a large mixing bowl and pour the green purée over it. Place the salt, cloves, bay leaf, oregano, cumin, coriander and black pepper in a spice grinder and grind to a fine powder. Sprinkle the ground spices over the pork. Mix together with your hands and leave to marinate in the refrigerator for at least 12 hours.

Continued...

4. When you're ready to cook, set a large frying pan over a medium heat and add the marinated pork mixture. Cook, stirring frequently, for about 10 minutes, and taste to check the seasoning – adjust the salt, pepper and spices to your taste.

5. Take the pork off the heat and set aside. Warm a generous slick of oil in a clean frying pan and, when hot, add the duck eggs. Keep basting the top side of the eggs with the oil, ensuring they are evenly cooked.

6. To serve, place 2 tostadas side by side on each plate and put a tablespoon of pork on each tostada, followed by a duck egg on top. Sprinkle over the queso fresco and some coriander leaves, add breddos hot sauce to your taste, and serve with lemon wedges.

CRUNCHY NUT FRIED SWEETBREADS & WILD GARLIC AIOLI

INGREDIENTS

SERVES 4

250g (9oz) lamb sweetbreads
550ml (1 pint/generous 2½ cups)
    whole milk
500ml (18fl oz/2 cups) rapeseed oil,
    for frying
120g (4oz/1 cup) plain (all-purpose) flour
100ml (3½fl oz/scant ½ cup) buttermilk
200g (7oz/2½ cups) panko breadcrumbs
    or good-quality breadcrumbs
50g (1¾oz/½ cup) almonds, finely chopped
50g (1¾oz/½ cup) sesame seeds
8 corn tortillas (see page 43)

For the aïoli:

1 bunch of wild garlic, finely chopped
sea salt and freshly ground black pepper
2 large, free-range egg yolks
½ teaspoon English or Dijon mustard
1 teaspoon white wine vinegar
250ml (9fl oz/1 cup) sunflower oil
    or rapeseed oil

1. To prepare the sweetbreads, soak them in the milk overnight. Once you've done this, you'll need to remove the membrane surrounding them (it's a bit like skinning a sausage, a bit fiddly but a necessary process).

2. Make the aïoli following the method on page 114, substituting wild garlic for the garlic and adding it in at the end.

3. Heat the oil in a deep heavy-based pan to 190°C (375°F). Place the flour in a bowl, the buttermilk in a second bowl, and the panko breadcrumbs, almonds and sesame seeds in a third bowl. Dip your sweetbreads first in the flour, then in the buttermilk and finally, in the panko breadcrumbs. Drop them into the pan of oil in batches. Fry for around 4 minutes, or use a temperature probe, ensuring that the temperature has reached 70°C (155°F) in the centre of the sweetbread.

4. Serve with the aïoli on a tortilla.

BUTTERMILK LAMB WITH SPRING GREENS, SALSA VERDE & YOGHURT

INGREDIENTS

SERVES 4

1 leg of lamb, deboned and butterflied

For the marinade:
1 litre (1¾ pints/4 cups) buttermilk
1 tablespoon sea salt
juice of 2 lemons
8 garlic cloves, crushed
1 tablespoon freshly ground black pepper
leaves from 2 sprigs of rosemary,
*   finely chopped*
2 tablespoons Dijon mustard

For the spring greens:
500g (1lb 2oz) spring greens,
*   finely chopped*
50g (1¾oz) butter
3 garlic cloves, finely sliced
juice of 1 lemon
1 teaspoon each of sea salt and freshly
*   ground black pepper*

To serve:
2 x Dong's flatbreads (see page 41)
100ml (3½fl oz/scant ½ cup) yoghurt
100ml (3½fl oz/scant ½ cup) shack salsa
*   verde (see page 118)*
seeds from 1 pomegranate

1. Mix all the marinade ingredients together in a large dish and, once fully incorporated, add the lamb. Mix thoroughly. Cover and marinate for 24 hours in the refrigerator.

2. When you're ready to cook, drain the lamb from the marinade and preheat your oven to 160°C (300°F/ Gas 2). Place your lamb in a roasting tray in the oven for 1½ hours, then turn the oven temperature up to 200°C (400°F/Gas 6) and cook for a further 20 minutes to crisp up the lamb. Remove from the oven and set aside to rest for 15 minutes.

3. Cook the spring greens in a pan of boiling water for 3 minutes. Remove and drain. Melt the butter in a frying pan over a medium heat, add the garlic and cook for 3 minutes, then add the spring greens, lemon juice and salt and pepper. Remove from the heat and set aside.

4. Warm up the flatbreads in a frying pan for 2 minutes on each side. Pull the lamb apart and place on the flatbreads. Move them to a serving platter and add the spring greens. Drizzle over the yoghurt and salsa verde and scatter over the pomegranate seeds.

TUNA TOSTADA, CHIPOTLE MAYONNAISE, BUTTER BRAISED JALAPENOS & AVOCADO

INGREDIENTS

SERVES 4

For the tuna:
500g (1lb 2oz) sashimi-grade tuna,
    sliced across the grain into roughly
    60g (2¼oz) portions
juice of 4 limes

For the soy glaze:
100ml (3½fl oz/scant ½ cup) soy sauce
100ml (3½fl oz/scant ½ cup) sake
100ml (3½fl oz/scant ½ cup) mirin
100g (3½oz/½ cup) granulated sugar
2 teaspoons cornflour (cornstarch)
1 tablespoon water

For the jalapeños:
50g (1¾oz) unsalted butter
3 jalapeño chillies, sliced thinly into rings

To serve:
8 tostadas (see page 40)
4 teaspoons chipotle mayonnaise
    (see page 116)
1 avocado, sliced
1 tablespoon white sesame seeds
1 lime, quartered

This recipe takes inspiration from one of our favourite restaurants, Contramar, in Mexico City. It is the perfect lunch spot, serving uber-fresh seafood nestled away in the Roma district. Its tuna tostada is unforgettable for those who have visited.

1. To make the soy glaze, combine the soy sauce, sake, mirin and sugar in a pan and cook on a medium heat for 3 minutes. Mix the cornflour and water in a small bowl, add to the soy mix and stir until thickened. Remove from the heat.

2. To make the jalapeños, put the butter into a pan with the jalapeños and cook on a low heat for 5 minutes. Remove and set aside.

3. Put 2 tostadas on each serving plate. Place ½ teaspoon of chipotle mayonnaise and a slice of avocado on each tostada.

4. Put the tuna into a bowl and pour over the lime juice, mixing it through to ensure all the pieces are covered. Take 2 slices of tuna, dip into the soy glaze, then place on each tostada. Place a few jalapeños on each slice of tuna and sprinkle over some sesame seeds.

5. Give the tostadas a further squirt of lime juice and serve.

SALT-BAKED TROUT WITH LIME & WATERCRESS

INGREDIENTS

SERVES 4

2 trout, gutted and cleaned
4 sprigs of thyme
2 sprigs of rosemary
4 garlic cloves, peeled
2 limes, finely sliced

For the salt crust:
3kg (6lb 8oz/11 cups) fine sea salt
100ml (3½fl oz/scant ½ cup) water
4 egg whites

To serve:
8 tostadas (see page 40)
100g (3½oz) watercress
chilli flakes
12 cherry tomatoes, halved
100ml (3½fl oz/scant ½ cup) Greek yoghurt
1 lime, quartered

If you've never salt-baked a fish, I strongly encourage you to do so now. The salt intensifies the sweetness of the fish and acts as a casing in which the fish steams.

1. Stuff the cavity of each trout with the thyme, rosemary and garlic and a lime each.

2. Preheat your oven to 200°C (400°F/ Gas 6). You need two baking trays, big enough to hold a trout each. Line each baking tray with baking (parchment) paper. Place the salt in a bowl, add the water to dampen, then mix in the egg whites. You're looking for a clay-like texture. Divide the mixture in half. Place half of each mixture onto each baking tray and then place the trouts on top of the salt. Cover the trouts with the remaining salt, ensuring that they are completely covered. Sprinkle more water over the salt to dampen.

3. Bake the fish in the preheated oven for 40 minutes. To make sure they're cooked, prod a skewer through the crust and into the fish. It should come out hot to the touch. When the fish are cooked, take them out of the oven and crack open the crust. Carefully remove the fish whole and set aside, or remove the fish flesh to serve.

4. To assemble the dish, place a forkful of trout on each tostada, followed by some watercress, chilli flakes, tomatoes, yoghurt and lime wedges.

SCALLOP AGUACHILE

INGREDIENTS

SERVES 4 AS A SNACK

4 fresh scallops
1 red onion, very finely sliced and soaked
   in ice-cold water for 10 minutes
2 teaspoons dried chilli flakes, to serve
8 tostadas (see page 40)

For the marinade:
juice of 1 lime
2 tablespoons orange juice
2 tablespoons grapefruit juice
1 teaspoon mezcal (optional)
1 teaspoon sea salt
2 tablespoons chopped coriander
   (cilantro)
2 tablespoons deseeded and finely
   diced cucumber

*You can use the marinade for this
aguachile on most firm white fish, as
long as it's extremely fresh.*

1. In a pestle and mortar, combine all the marinade ingredients.

2. Shuck the scallops and discard the orange coral. Wash the white muscle and slice it in half horizontally, and then again, so you double the number of scallop pieces. In a serving dish, layer the scallops over the marinade.

3. Sprinkle the onion and chilli flakes over the scallops. Place a couple of tostadas by each plate to serve.

CRAB TOSTADA, ARBOL & TARRAGON

INGREDIENTS

SERVES 4

1 x 454g (1lb) tub of freshly picked
    white crabmeat
1 small cucumber, deseeded and
    finely chopped
1 bunch of chervil, finely chopped
1 bunch of tarragon, finely chopped
grated zest of 1 lemon
2 tablespoons mayonnaise
1 teaspoon wholegrain mustard
1 tablespoon poppy seeds
a pinch of chilli flakes
2 teaspoons butter, melted
8 tostadas (see page 40)
2 limes, quartered
breddos hot sauce (see page 110), to taste
a few sprigs coriander (cilantro), to serve

1. Sift through the crab to ensure that there's no shell in there. Put it into a bowl and combine with the cucumber, chervil, tarragon and lemon zest.

2. In another bowl stir together the mayonnaise and mustard. Add the crabmeat mixture, along with the poppy seeds and chilli flakes, and combine.

3. Spoon some melted butter onto a tostada and put the crabmeat on top. Serve with a wedge of lime, some breddos hot sauce and some coriander.

BAJA FISH TACO

INGREDIENTS

SERVES 4

For the batter:
200g (7oz/1⅓ cups) rice flour
100g (3½oz/¾ cup) plain (all-purpose)
    flour
1 egg, beaten
1 teaspoon baking powder
1 teaspoon fine salt
1 teaspoon chilli powder
½ teaspoon dried oregano
200ml (7fl oz/scant 1 cup) cold sparkling
    water or light beer

For the fish:
500ml (18fl oz/2 cups) rapeseed oil,
    for frying
1 large pollack fillet, skinned and
    pin boned, cut into 8 evenly sized
    rectangular pieces
100g (3½oz/¾ cups) rice flour

To serve:
8 corn tortillas (see page 43)
100g (3½oz/scant ½ cup) lime aïoli
    (see page 114; use lime juice instead
    of vinegar)
½ head white cabbage, finely chopped
100g (3½oz/scant ½ cup) pico de gallo
    (see page 109)
1 jalapeño chilli, finely sliced
a handful of coriander (cilantro),
    leaves picked
cascabel chilli salt (see page 117)
4 limes, halved

Chris and I travelled the coast of Baja California in 2015, eating the best fish tacos known to man. They were so cheap, with fish fresh from the sea, coated in a crunchy light batter, then garnished with shredded cabbage and a choice of zingy, spicy and refreshing salsas. Years of cooking fish tacos had given the taqueros an instinctive knack for cooking the fish perfectly every time. While not a like-for-like copy, our take uses the best of British produce to recreate a Baja classic.

1. Heat the rapeseed oil in a deep heavy-based pan to 190°C (375°F).

2. To make the batter, mix together all the ingredients except the sparkling water or beer. Slowly pour in the sparkling water or beer and whisk until you have a batter-like consistency; ignore any lumps.

3. Dip one piece of fish at a time into the rice flour. Using tongs, dip the fish into the batter and then gently place the fish in the hot oil. Be sure to put the fish into the oil away from your body in case of oil splashes. Repeat with 3 of the other pieces of fish and cook for 4 minutes.

4. Take the first 4 pieces out of the oil and leave to drain on kitchen paper. Repeat with the other 4 pieces of fish.

5. Assemble your tacos: warm the tortillas, then add a dollop of aïoli, followed by the fish, cabbage, pico de gallo, a couple of slices of jalapeño and some coriander. Sprinkle with cascabel chilli salt and add a squeeze of lime juice.

CAULIFLOWER 'AL PASTOR', PINEAPPLE & PICKLED ONIONS

INGREDIENTS

SERVES 4

1 head of cauliflower
2 teaspoons ground hibiscus flowers
    (optional)

For the marinade:
100ml (3½fl oz/scant ½ cup) natural
    yoghurt
2 garlic cloves
2 tablespoons achiote paste
1 onion, roughly chopped
1 tablespoon cider vinegar
1 teaspoon cumin seeds
3 allspice berries
2 teaspoons sea salt
1 teaspoon crushed black pepper

For the habanero crema:
200ml (7fl oz/scant 1 cup) crema
    (see page 109) or sour cream
2 chipotles in adobo (see page 37)
1 dried habanero chilli, soaked in hot water
    for 30 minutes
1 teaspoon dried oregano

1. To make the habanero crema, whiz all of the ingredients together in a blender until you have a smooth sauce.

2. Split the cauliflower in half vertically, core, then trim it at the base, leaving behind some of the root to keep the florets together.

3. In a bowl, whisk together the marinade ingredients until thoroughly combined. Rub the marinade mixture into the cauliflower, being sure to completely cover the two halves. Set aside to marinate for 3–4 hours.

4. Heat your oven to 220°C (425°F/Gas 7). Put the cauliflower halves on a baking tray, cut sides down, and bake in the oven for 1–1½ hours. Take out of the oven, sprinkle the hibiscus powder over the cauliflower and slice into 4cm (1½ inch) segments.

Continued...

To serve:

8 corn tortillas (see page 43)
½ teaspoon ancho chilli oil (see page 113),
    or to taste
pink pickled onions (see page 64)
4 radishes, halved
½ pineapple, sliced into sticks, roasted
    in a dry frying pan or chargrill pan
    until blackened

5. Warm up your tortillas and place some of the cauliflower segments on each one. Follow with the habanero crema, ancho chilli oil, pink pickled onions, radishes and pineapple sticks.

LEMON SOLE CEVICHE WITH ARBOL, GRAPEFRUIT & RED ONION

INGREDIENTS

SERVES 4

600g (1lb 5oz) lemon sole, skinned and trimmed
sea salt
100ml (3½fl oz/scant ½ cup) leche de tigre (tiger's milk) (see below)
1 large red onion, very finely sliced and soaked in ice-cold water for 5 minutes
a few coriander (cilantro) sprigs, leaves finely chopped
½ grapefruit, segmented, peeled and cut into 1cm (½ inch) cubes
1 jalapeño chilli, deseeded and finely chopped
1 chile de árbol, finely sliced
4 tostadas (see page 40)
1 lime, quartered

For the leche de tigre (tiger's milk):

1cm (½ inch) piece of peeled ginger, cut into quarters
2 small garlic cloves
8 sprigs of coriander (cilantro), roughly chopped
juice of 16 limes
1 teaspoon sea salt
4 teaspoons chilli paste

1. To make the leche de tigre, combine everything apart from the chilli paste in a bowl and stir to infuse. Strain into a second bowl and add the salt. Stir in the chilli paste and mix well.

2. Cut the fish into uniform strips of around 4 x 3cm (1½ x 1¼ inches). Place in a large bowl, add a good pinch of salt and mix together gently with a metal spoon. Leave this for a minute, then pour over the tiger's milk and combine gently with the spoon. Leave the fish to 'cook' in this marinade for another minute.

3. Add the drained onions, coriander, grapefruit and jalapeño and árbol chillies to the fish. Mix together gently with the spoon.

4. Place a tostada on each plate and spoon in some lemon sole ceviche. Serve with lime.

SPICED CHESTNUT MUSHROOM, PORCINI, TRUFFLE, WALNUTS & BURNT SPRING ONION CREMA

INGREDIENTS

SERVES 4

1 tablespoon cayenne pepper
1 tablespoon smoked paprika
a pinch of sea salt and freshly ground
*   black pepper*
a pinch of sugar
20g (¾oz) dried porcini mushrooms
250g (9oz/2 cups) chestnut mushrooms
1 tablespoon rapeseed oil
50g (1¾oz/¼ cup) walnuts, crushed
1 teaspoon truffle oil

To serve:
4 corn tortillas (see page 43)
4 teaspoons pico de gallo (see page 109)
breddos hot sauce (see page 110), to taste
2 tablespoons burnt spring onion crema
*   (see page 113)*
finely chopped coriander (cilantro)
4 radishes, sliced
1 lime, quartered

1. In a bowl, mix together the cayenne pepper and smoked paprika, add a pinch of salt and pepper and a small pinch of sugar. Set aside.

2. Put the dried porcini mushrooms into a bowl or cup and pour boiling water over them, then leave them to brew for 10 minutes.

3. Cut the chestnut mushrooms into slices. Heat the oil in a pan and, when it's hot, add the chestnut mushrooms and drained porcini (reserve the liquid) and stir and flip to ensure they are all coated in the oil. Add the dry spice mix, making sure the mushrooms are well coated in the now flavoured oil. Once the mushrooms have started to cook down and gain colour, add the crushed walnuts and a dash of the porcini soaking juices, as this will add to the intensity. Finish with the truffle oil.

4. Fill your tortillas with the mushroom mix. Add some pico de gallo and a splash of the hot sauce. Add some crema over the top and finally garnish with coriander, radishes and a squeeze of lime.

TEMPURA VEGETABLES, LIME AIOLI & EPAZOTE

INGREDIENTS

SERVES 4

For the batter:

100g (3½oz/¾ cup) rice flour
1 egg, beaten
160ml (5fl oz/⅔ cup) cold sparkling water
    or light beer
1 tablespoon sesame seeds or poppy seeds
1 teaspoon chilli flakes, plus extra to serve
½ teaspoon epazote (see page 37), plus
    extra to serve

For the vegetables:

200ml (7fl oz/scant 1 cup) rapeseed oil
4 baby beetroot (beet), peeled and cut
    into 5mm (¼ inch) wedges
4 baby carrots, peeled and halved
4 baby leeks, washed
8 kale leaves, cut into roughly 8cm
    (3¼ inch) squares
a handful of fennel tops
4 slices of pumpkin, roughly 5mm (¼ inch)
    thick and 8cm (3¼ inches) long
4 white mushrooms
salt and freshly ground black pepper

To serve:

8 corn tortillas (see page 43)
4 tablespoons lime aïoli (see page 113)
1 tablespoon coriander oil (see page 117)

1. In a bowl, whisk together the rice flour and egg, then pour in the water or beer. Try to keep it smooth. Add the sesame seeds or poppy seeds, chilli flakes and epazote.

2. Heat the rapeseed oil to 180°C (355°F). Dip the vegetables into the tempura batter using tongs, then lower them carefully into the hot oil in batches. Cook for 3–4 minutes, until golden, and remove with a slotted spoon to a tray lined with kitchen paper. Season with sea salt and some black pepper. Repeat until you have fried all of the vegetables.

3. Warm up your tortillas and place vegetables on each, followed by a big spoonful of lime aïoli, a sprinkling of chilli flakes, a little epazote and a drizzle of coriander oil.

SALSAS A
C

NDIMENTS

SMOKY STEAK MARINADE

MAKES 300ML (10½OZ/1¼ CUPS)

*1 head of garlic, cloves separated
  and peeled*
¼ onion, peeled
3–4 spring onions (scallions), chopped
*2 tablespoons chipotle chilli powder or
  smoked paprika*
3 chipotles in adobo (see page 37)
1 tablespoon freshly ground black pepper
2 jalapeño chillies
½ bunch of coriander (cilantro)
180ml (6fl oz/¾ cup) beer
juice and grated zest of 1 orange
juice and grated zest of 1 grapefruit
juice and grated zest of 3 limes
*1 tablespoon each of sea salt and
  freshly ground black pepper*
1 tablespoon sugar
2 tablespoons rapeseed or groundnut oil

1. Put everything in a blender and blitz
to a paste.

CHIPOTLE CASHEW NUT SALSA

**MAKES AROUND 300G
(10½OZ/1¼ CUPS)**

200g (7oz/1¾ cups) salted cashew nuts
*4 tablespoons chipotles in adobo
  (see page 37)*
4 tablespoons water
juice of 1 lime

1. Roast the cashews in a dry pan until
aromatic, for about 2 minutes.

2. Put all the ingredients into a blender and
pulse until you have a rough salsa with the
consistency of wholegrain mustard. You're
looking for a smoky and spicy flavour. Store
in an airtight jar for up to 2 weeks.

PICO DE GALLO

MAKES 400G (14OZ/SCANT 2 CUPS)

300g (10½oz) ripe vine tomatoes
2 medium red onions, diced
½ bunch of coriander (cilantro),
*   finely chopped*
½ jalapeño chilli, deseeded and
*   finely chopped*
1 teaspoon sea salt
1 teaspoon freshly ground black pepper
1 teaspoon sugar
juice of 2–3 limes
1 teaspoon rapeseed oil

1. First quarter the tomatoes. Remove the cores, then dice the tomatoes into 5mm (¼ inch) cubes and put them into a large bowl.

2. Add the red onions to the bowl with the coriander and jalapeños. Add the salt and pepper and taste to check the seasoning.

3. Once you're happy with the flavour, mix in the sugar. Add lime juice, to taste, and the oil. Stir to combine and taste again; the mixture should be salty, sweet, zingy and slightly spicy. If you like your salsas hot, replace the jalapeño with a Scotch bonnet or habanero.

HOMEMADE CREMA

MAKES 250ML (9FL OZ/1 CUP)

200ml (7fl oz/scant 1 cup) organic
*   double (heavy) cream*
1½ tablespoons organic buttermilk

Crema is a kind of Mexican sour cream/ crème fraîche hybrid. It's not difficult to make and the taste is far superior to anything you'll get from normal sour cream or crème fraîche.

1. Heat the double cream in a pan to 35°C (95°F), take off the heat and pour into a glass jar. Add the buttermilk, place the lid on the jar loosely and store in a warm place for 24 hours. Then tighten the lid and store in the fridge.

BREDDOS HOT SAUCE

MAKES 400ML
(14FL OZ/SCANT 2 CUPS)

2–3 Scotch bonnet chillies
small pinch of sea salt
2 large tablespoons sugar
juice of 4 limes
1½ x 400g (14oz) tins of peeled plum
*   tomatoes*
a handful of coriander (cilantro), chopped

We highly recommend wearing silicone
kitchen gloves when making this recipe.

1. Remove the stalks and quarter the Scotch bonnets. If you want to reduce the heat of the sauce, remove the seeds at this stage. Put the Scotch bonnets into a blender and blitz.

2. Add the salt and sugar and squeeze in the lime juice. Blitz again for a moment. Add the tomatoes and coriander and blitz again.

3. The tomato taste should fall into the background, with sweet citrus flavours coming through and building, with quite a long-lasting heat.

REFRIED BEANS

MAKES 400G (14OZ/2 CUPS)

4 tablespoons rapeseed oil,
*   plus 2 more tablespoons*
1 large onion, diced
3 garlic cloves, toasted with their skins
*   on until black spots appear, then*
*   peeled and minced*
1 teaspoon epazote (see page 37)
1 teaspoon Mexican oregano
1 teaspoon ground coriander
1 teaspoon ground cumin
1 teaspoon chipotle powder
1 tablespoon Maldon salt
400g (14oz/2 cups) dried pinto beans
*   (washed under cold running water)*
*   or 1 tin of canned pinto beans*

1. Add the 4 tablespoons of oil to a medium-sized pot and heat. Add the onions and cook gently, stirring often, about 10 minutes.

2. Add the garlic, herbs, spices and salt and cook for another 3 minutes, then add the pinto beans and, after a minute, cover with water (if using dried beans).

3. If using canned beans, cook for another 10 minutes and go to step 5.

4. Bring to a boil. Reduce to a high simmer and cook the beans for around 1–2 hours. Drain, reserving a cup of the liquid.

5. Whizz the beans to a paste in a blender.

6. In another pot, heat the extra oil. Once hot, add the beans. Re-fry for 3–4 minutes, adding some of the reserved bean cooking liquid if the mixture is too thick.

GUACAMOLE

MAKES 400G (14OZ/SCANT 2 CUPS)

4 or 5 jalapeño chillies
½ bunch of coriander (cilantro)
6 ripe avocados
1 tablespoon rapeseed oil
sea salt and freshly ground black pepper
juice of 3 limes

We use this guacamole as the base for a
number of sauces in our kitchen, and the
purity of the recipe relies on your sourcing
the best, ripest avocados you can find.
If you're preparing the guacamole in
advance, put the stones back into the
avocado mix – this will prevent oxidization.

1. Deseed the jalapeños, then very finely
chop them and the coriander.

2. Slice your avocados through the middle
and split. Take out the stones and set aside
(they'll be useful later). Scoop out the
flesh of the avocado, place on a chopping
board and add the oil. Taking a fork, mash
the avocados into a rough paste, making
sure you retain a decent amount of
texture. Throw the chopped chillies and
coriander into the mix and season. Fold all
the ingredients together using the fork,
ensuring that they're evenly distributed.
Once you've done this, squeeze the lime
juice over the top and mix through.

MANGO, LIME & HABANERO SALSA

MAKES 200G (7OZ/1 CUP)

1 mango, cut into small cubes
juice of 2 limes
1 habanero chilli
a handful of coriander (cilantro)
  leaves, chopped
a handful of mint leaves, chopped
a pinch of sea salt
a pinch of sugar
1 teaspoon olive oil

1. Mix all the ingredients together and
store in the fridge until needed.

PICKLED HABANEROS

MAKES 100G (3½OZ/½ CUP)

*200ml (7fl oz/scant 1 cup) apple
    cider vinegar*
2 tablespoons sugar
1½ teaspoons Maldon sea salt
100g (3½oz) habanero chillies
1 tablespoon mustard seeds

1. Bring the apple cider vinegar to a
simmer in a pan and mix in the sugar and
salt. While this is simmering, slice the
habaneros into concentric rings. You can
remove the seeds to decrease the heat,
though they'll still be very hot. Place the
chillies and mustard seeds in a Mason or
pickling jar (or just an old jam jar) and pour
over the vinegar mix. Leave to pickle for a
few days before using.

AVOCADO MOJO

MAKES 300ML (10½FL OZ/1¼ CUPS)

1 quantity of guacamole (see page 111)
3 garlic cloves, finely chopped
1 tablespoon roasted garlic oil (page 119)
1 jalapeño chilli
1 teaspoon dried oregano
juice of 1 lime
a handful of coriander (cilantro)
1 teaspoon chilli flakes
sea salt and freshly ground black pepper

1. Place all the ingredients in a blender and
pulse. You may need to scrape down the
sides of the jug and add some water if the
mojo is too thick.

ANCHO CHILLI OIL

**MAKES ABOUT 1 LITRE
(1¾ PINTS/4 CUPS)**

*5 garlic cloves
20 ancho chillies
4 sprigs of rosemary
2 sprigs of thyme
1 litre (1¾ pints/4 cups) olive oil*

1. Put all the ingredients into a pan and cook over a medium heat until you see bubbles forming. Turn the heat down and continue to cook for a further 20 minutes. Remove from the heat and leave to steep for 2 hours.

2. Strain the oil through a fine sieve into a bottle, pressing down on all the solids to extract their flavour.

BURNT SPRING ONION CREMA

MAKES 250ML (9FL OZ/1 CUP)

*2 bunches of spring onions (scallions)
200ml (7fl oz/scant 1 cup) crema (see
    page 109) or sour cream*

1. Clean the spring onions and trim the root and tips. Use a griddle pan, or better still a barbecue, and get it nice and hot. If using a griddle pan, wipe the surface with some plain cooking oil (rapeseed works well), and place the spring onions on a medium to high heat. Let the onions sit so that they get nicely blackened, turning them from time to time.

2. Once the onions are ready, blitz them with the crema or sour cream and you'll have a lovely complement to some of our more savoury tacos, such as the short-rib or the mushroom.

AIOLI

MAKES 250G (9OZ/1¼ CUPS)

2 small garlic cloves, peeled
sea salt and freshly ground black pepper
2 large free-range egg yolks
½ teaspoon English or Dijon mustard
1 teaspoon white wine vinegar (or lime juice
to make a lime aïoli)
250ml (9fl oz/1 cup) sunflower or
rapeseed oil

1. Crush the garlic to a paste with a pinch of sea salt, then thoroughly combine in a bowl with the egg yolks, mustard, vinegar or lime juice and some pepper. In a slow steady stream, whisk the oil into the egg mix to properly emulsify. By the time you've added all the oil, you should have a thick, glossy, wobbly aïoli that holds its shape.

2. Taste and add more salt, pepper, mustard or vinegar/lime juice if you like. If it seems too thick, stir in a tablespoon or two of warm water to let it down.

HABANERO AIOLI

MAKES 400G (14OZ/SCANT 2 CUPS)

5 dried habanero chillies, soaked in hot
water to soften
1 teaspoon Mexican oregano
1 quantity aioli (see left)

1. Blend the habaneros and oregano in a food processor or blender until you have a smooth paste. Add the aïoli and blend again until incorporated.

TOMATILLO SALSA

MAKES 800G (1LB 12OZ/4 CUPS)

2 jalapeño chillies, roughly chopped
2 large garlic cloves, peeled and crushed
1kg (2lb 4oz) fresh tomatillos, husked,
*   washed and sliced in half*
1 shallot
½ avocado, stoned and diced
2 tablespoons coriander (cilantro)
*   leaves, chopped*
juice of 1 lime
½ teaspoon sea salt

If you want to ramp up the smokiness in
this dish, roast the tomatillos in a dry pan
until blackened, then blend.

1. Place the jalapeños, garlic, tomatillos and shallot in a blender and pulse until smooth. Add the avocado and some water if the mixture is too thick. Fold in the coriander, lime juice and salt.

SALTED CHILLI PASTE

MAKES 100G (3½OZ/¼ CUP)

15 long red chillies
5 bird's-eye chillies
2 tablespoons sea salt
5 garlic cloves
1 tablespoon apple cider vinegar

1. Pulse all the ingredients in a blender until you have a rough paste. Place in a sterilized glass jar and seal. Stir daily for a week, after which the paste will be slightly fermented and ready to use.

CHIPOTLE MAYONNAISE

MAKES 275G (9¾OZ/SCANT 1½ CUPS)

*2 chipotles in adobo (see page 37),
    with 2 tablespoons of the sauce*
1 tablespoon water
*1 quantity aïoli (see page 114), omitting
    the garlic*

1. Blend the chipotles with the water and
the adobo sauce until a smooth paste
forms. Add the aïoli and blitz on high
speed until incorporated.

X NI PEK MAYAN SALSA

MAKES 400G (14OZ/SCANT 2 CUPS)

*3 red onions, very finely sliced and soaked
    in ice-cold water for 10 minutes*
*5 tablespoons freshly squeezed
    orange juice*
1 tablespoon grapefruit juice
juice of 4 limes
*½ habanero, deseeded, deveined
    and finely chopped*

*X ni pek literally means hot as a dog's nose,
and is all about curing red onions in citrus,
which effectively cuts through the richness
of the cochinita pibil pork.*

1. Drain the onions and put in a bowl.
Pour over the orange, grapefruit and
lime juices and add the chilli. Leave the
onions to 'cook' in the citric acid for about
an hour. They're ready when they turn a
vivid pink colour.

CASCABEL CHILLI SALT

MAKES 50G (1¾OZ/¼ CUP)

6 dried cascabel chillies
3 tablespoons sea salt
1 teaspoon smoked paprika

1. Toast the chillies in a frying pan over a medium heat for a couple of minutes.

2. Once cool, put into a spice grinder or pestle and mortar and grind to a fine powder. Mix in the salt and smoked paprika.

CORIANDER OIL

MAKES 400ML (14FL OZ/1¾ CUPS)

200g (7oz) coriander (cilantro) leaves
400ml (14fl oz/1¾ cups) olive oil

1. Fill a bowl with ice-cold water. Bring some water to the boil in a small pan and drop in the coriander leaves. Blanch for 5 seconds, then drain and place immediately in the ice-cold water.

2. Once the leaves are cool, after about 5 minutes, squeeze them dry and place them in a pan with the olive oil. Cook over a medium heat until the oil starts to bubble very slightly or reaches 60°C (140°F). Take off the heat and let cool, then strain into a blender and whizz on high speed. Store in a dark place to ensure the oil keeps its colour.

SHACK SALSA VERDE

MAKES 400G (14OZ/2 SCANT CUPS)

75g (3oz) parsley, chopped
25g (1oz) coriander (cilantro), chopped
1 tablespoon roughly chopped garlic
100g (3½oz) spring onions (scallions),
*   chopped*
1 bunch of fresh thyme, chopped
125ml (4fl oz/½ cup) water
2 teaspoons grated lime zest
6 tablespoons fresh lime juice
1 Scotch bonnet chilli, cut in half
*   and deseeded*
1 tablespoon sea salt
1 tablespoon fresh peeled and
*   chopped ginger*
375ml (13fl oz/1½ cups) olive oil

1. Place all the ingredients apart from the olive oil in a blender and pulse on high. Reduce the speed and slowly add the olive oil until emulsified.

ADOBO

MAKES 200G (7OZ/SCANT 1 CUP)

6 ancho chillies, deseeded and deveined
6 guajillo chillies, deseeded and deveined
75g (3oz) canned chipotle chillies
4 garlic cloves, roasted
250ml (9fl oz/1 cup) cider vinegar
½ teaspoon Mexican oregano
1 teaspoon black peppercorns
½ teaspoon cumin seeds, toasted
½ teaspoon cloves, toasted
1cm (½ inch) stick of cinnamon or
*   ½ teaspoon ground cinnamon*
cinnamon powder

1. In a non-stick pan over a high flame, toast the ancho and guajillo chillies until they begin to blister, then soak them in warm water for about 25 minutes, until soft and malleable.

2. Remove the chillies and discard the soaking water. Put the soaked chillies into a blender with the remaining ingredients and purée until smooth. Transfer the mixture to a bowl and stir thoroughly with a rubber spatula. Keep refrigerated.

ROASTED GARLIC OIL

MAKES 400ML (14FL OZ/1¾ CUPS)

*3 heads of garlic, cloves, separated and
    peeled*
1 sprig of thyme
1 sprig of rosemary
400ml (14fl oz/1¾ cups) olive oil

1. Toast the garlic in a dry frying pan until
blackened. Add the thyme, rosemary and
oil and cook on a very low heat for 30
minutes. Remove from the heat and cool.
Store in an airtight container.

HABANERO OR SCOTCH BONNET SALSA

MAKES 200ML (7FL OZ/SCANT 1 CUP)

*10 habanero or Scotch bonnet chillies,
    destemmed and deseeded*
1 tablespoon olive oil
1 white onion, chopped
100ml (3½fl oz/scant ½ cup) orange juice
1 teaspoon grated orange zest
*1 tablespoon lime juice and 1 teaspoon
    grated lime zest*
75ml (3fl oz/scant ⅓ cup) cider vinegar
a pinch of Mexican oregano
3½ tablespoons sugar
75ml (3fl oz/scant ⅓ cup) water
1 tablespoon sea salt

1. Toast the chillies in a dry pan until
blackened. Remove and set aside. Heat
the oil in the same pan and add the onion.
Fry over a low heat until soft, about
7 minutes.

2. Put all the ingredients into a blender
or food processor and blend to a coarse
purée. Transfer the mixture to a saucepan
over a low heat and simmer gently for
30 minutes. Remove the salsa from the
heat and let cool to room temperature.
Store in the fridge in an airtight container.

Managing Director **Sarah Lavelle**
Commissioning Editor **Stacey Cleworth**
Project Editor **Sofie Shearman**
Designers **Alexander Green & Emily Lapworth**
Food & Reportage Photographer **Kris Kirkham**
Head of Production **Stephen Lang**
Production Controller **Gary Hayes**

Published in 2024 by Quadrille,
an imprint of Hardie Grant Publishing

Quadrille
52–54 Southwark Street
London SE1 1UN
quadrille.com

Text © Nud Dudhia & Chris Whitney 2024
All photography © Kris Kirkham 2016, except for pages
    21, 29 and 30 © Nud Dudhia 2016

Text is extracted and updated from *breddos Tacos* by Nud Dudhia
& Chris Whitney.

Cataloguing in Publication Data: a catalogue record for this book is
available from the British Library.

978 1 83783 166 1

Printed in China